Derek Tangye has become famous all over the world for his series of bestsellers about his flower farm in Cornwall. The series, which began with A GULL ON THE ROOF, describes a simple way of life which thousands of his readers would like to adopt themselves.

Derek and his wife left their glamorous existence in London when they discovered Minack, a deserted cottage close to the cliffs of Mount's Bay. Jeannie gave up her job as Press Relations Officer of the Savoy Hotel Group and Derek Tangye resigned from MI5. They then proceeded to carve from the wild land around the cottage the meadows which became their flower farm.

A Cornish Summer

DEREK TANGYE

Sketches by Jean Tangye

SPHERE BOOKS LIMITED

First published in Great Britain by Michael Joseph Ltd 1970
First published in paperback by New English Library Ltd 1972
Copyright © by Derek Tangye 1970
Published by Sphere Books Ltd 1984
27 Wrights Lane, London W8 5TZ
Reprinted 1985, 1987

To Amanda Vyvyan

TRADE
MARK

Printed and bound in Great Britain by
Cox & Wyman Ltd, Reading

ONE

When did it happen? Three, five, ten summers ago?
Incidents merge into each other leaving timeless intervals.
I do not remember the summer when the drought dried up
Monty's Leap, or the summer when I killed an adder outside
our door, or the summer when a hoopoe paraded on the
grass in front of the cottage, or the summer when I caught a
conger eel in my lobster pot, and scared Jeannie when I
brought it to her in the kitchen. Important incidents at the
time, they have faded into one summer; so too have the
pleasant hours I have watched Lama, the little black cat,
and Boris, the muscovy drake sitting incongruously side by
side, the one purring, the other ready to raise his head
feathers and hiss harmlessly the second he was disturbed; so

5

too have the stares of Penny and Fred the donkeys, looking down at us from the field above our porch, demanding our attention.

When did it happen? I do not know which summer it was when we watched the fox cubs playing in the field on the other side of the shallow valley, fearing that some stranger would see them too, and disturb them. All soft scented days when woodpigeons clapped their wings in courtship, when a raven grunted overhead, when green woodpeckers called to each other in the wood, belong to one summer; all still nights when voices of fishermen, a mile or more out to sea, sounded so loud that they were like ghosts talking in the front garden. There are no dates in my memory. No dates until this summer.

Our land stretches from a wood in one direction to the cliff and the rocks and the sea in the other. A community of gulls use our rocks as their home, and only when the easterlies blow from the Lizard do they go somewhere else. The southerlies, the northerlies, the westerlies, see them gathered side by side, young gulls and old, aimlessly watching the sea, dozing, like lazy holiday-makers.

When Jeannie and I first came to Minack this community of gulls spent their time on a great, sloping rock of blue elvin half a mile away to the south, roosting there at night as they do now at Minack.

High above this rock are the meadows we used to rent, years ago, for the growing of early potatoes. It was a period when we believed that an eldorado lay in the production of new potatoes. We grew them already on our own land, but we were greedy, and we imagined ourselves becoming the largest growers of new potatoes in West Cornwall, and so we rented these meadows. We loved them in the beginning, then grew to fear them; the ground was stony and in dry springs the potato plants refused to grow; and in wet springs when the plants were lush, a gale would come and scythe them, blackening the leaves so that only the useless stalks were left. We slaved in these meadows yet, because of this hard labour, a remnant of affection remains in our memories of the time we spent there. I walked around them the other day, and I found an old boot still lying in one of

6

the hedges . . . a boot which had to be cut from my foot after my rotovator had overturned and one of the tines had pierced my foot. The ancient construction of galvanised iron known as the pink hut, partly hidden by laurel, is still there . . . the pink hut where we used to sprout our potato seed, and where we once helped to nurse a badger back to health after it had been caught in a gin trap. And still I can see in my mind those who aided us in our work. St Just miners who came between shifts to pick up the potatoes, Geoffrey Semmens, fast shoveller from St Buryan who had to leave after one disastrous potato harvest but who for long has been back with us; and Jane, and Shelagh. I can see a picture of Jane on a blazing May afternoon, barefooted, fair hair falling over her shoulders, pausing from her task of scratching in the ground for potatoes, and picking up a long handled shovel, then waving it angrily at an aircraft over-head because, it was rumoured, it had a device which detected uranium . . . Jane who came to us when she was just fifteen, lived in a cottage edging the cliff nearby, and who hated progress. And I can see Shelagh, a year older than Jane, wistful, tragic little waif who would suddenly break the silence as we filled the potato baskets: 'Do you know there are only one hundred and ninety-nine shopping days to Christmas?' We would laugh.

Down below us as we laboured were the gulls. Summer days of blue seas, and fishing boats hurrying to Newlyn. A buzzard hovering. Swallows skimming the meadows as they flew in from the south. A fox's silhouette on the mound of what was the old quarry. There was a primitive and beautiful wildness about these meadows. What would Jane have done had she then known that a lighthouse was to be built adjacent to the great rock of blue elvin, and pylons carrying electricity lines were to cross the meadows, a hundred years too late for those who might have needed it? She would at any rate have understood why the gulls took a dislike to the white building, and to the electronic note of the fog signal; and moved to Minack rocks.

We like them there, except we are made to feel as tres-passers when we wish to be on the rocks ourselves. We reach the wicker gate at the top of our cliff and look down at our pocket meadows, then to the granite rocks (we are on the dividing line between granite and blue elvin) . . . and the gulls. Reason, of course, says it does not matter if we walk down the little winding path, past one meadow and another, past the palm tree I planted when my mother died, past the bottom meadow of all, until we reach the point when the gulls have observed us and are stirring, flapping wings in annoyance, a cry from one then from another, until a general commotion disturbs the rocks and the sea, and the gulls fly away squawking with irritation that humans have invaded their privacy. Reason says it is absurd to feel self-conscious because we have interrupted their rumination. We intend no harm. We are not foxes . . . for foxes sometimes slip from the bracken, bramble covered hideouts on the cliff, to slink away at nights to the rocks, the rush of the waves silencing any noise of their approach. The foxes snatch, and take their trophy away, so it is not on the rocks I find the left over feathers, but in some corner of our land.

One day I saw a vixen set out to raid the gulls in mid afternoon, a warm, May afternoon; and I supposed she behaved so recklessly because she was craving food for her cubs. I watched her, through the gaps of an ancient stone wall, advance towards the somnolent gulls, using the path we follow ourselves. She had no cover as soon as she reached the top of the rocks and, although she slid like a huge snake towards them, she didn't fool the gulls for a moment. Up they went into the sky, crying out their fury, and I watched them hovering above her until a half dozen peeled away from the rest and began diving at her while she crouched in bewilderment. After a while they grew tired of this baiting and some of the gulls settled on the sea while others flew off down the coast.

I expected the vixen to give up her adventure and return to the undergrowth, but she was undaunted by the disappearance of her intended victims. A pause, and she was off again and reaching the rocks she began to scour them like a scavenger, pushing her nose into this crevice and that, then finding nothing to satisfy her, she hopped from one rock to another until she arrived at the seaweed covered rocks which are only seen when the tide is low. I had moved

8

from my hiding place to secure a better view, and if she looked up she would have seen me. I watched her leap across a pool, then another pool, then run along the edge of the deep one where we bathe on hot summer days. She halted there for a moment and stared at the still water as if she had been startled by her own reflection . . . then on again until she reached a terrace of rocks that rose upwards, fifty feet or so, to the undergrowth. She was up and gone and out of sight within a minute. Nothing to show for her trouble when she returned to her cubs at the earth.

Did this happen three, five, ten summers ago? I do not remember.

Perhaps this summer I will remember . . .

TWO

I had seen the first swallows of the year the day the daffodil
harvest was over. I was standing late in the afternoon a few
yards away from the cottage on what is called the bridge.
The spot has no resemblance to a bridge, and it only received
its name because, when standing or sitting there, you have
a panoramic view before you . . . as if you were on the
bridge of a ship. On summer days we spend much idle time
on the bridge. We have levelled part of an old stone wall
with dark blue slate at table height, and we sit on a bench
in front of it. The wall is a wide one, and there is enough
room for a narrow strip of earth above the dark blue slate;
and this is encased in stone so that we have a flower bed as

well on the wall. We grow mignonette there every summer, and on still days and evenings the air is full of its sweet scent.

Behind us, as we gaze at the view, is a field where cows from our neighbour's farm, look inquisitively down at us. On the right is what looks like an old building without a roof, and it is where for many years we stored the coal. It is small in area, and growing out of the base of the stone walls are blackthorn, and in the summer the small green leaves cover the area like an umbrella. We have cleaned it up, and made flower beds where the coal used to lie in a heap, and have lily of the valley in one bed, cyclamen in another, Christmas roses in a third; and every year we sow night scented stock in all three of them. We have painted white wrought iron chairs and a table in the middle, and when it is hot in the summer we sit there in the shade; or when a breeze is blowing which makes the bridge too cool, we sit there because it is sheltered.

On the left is an ancient stone pig trough cornering the wall where we have the blue slate and the bed of mignonette. It is square, and massive and we heaved it there after finding it hidden in the undergrowth. Pigs drank from it in olden days and now we keep it filled with water for the birds; and the gulls who spend their days on the roof use it. Alongside is an escallonia bush which we planted over eight years ago, and after taking a long time to settle, is now growing at a pace. This evergreen with its shiny little leaves which scent, and pink flowers which bloom twice a year, is the home of small birds at night, and Jeannie has given it the fanciful name of Escallonia Towers. Then comes the path of grey chippings which leads downhill past the cottage, window-less this side except for the window of our tiny bedroom, to the space where a caller parks his car. Here is the old barn, clay binding the stones of the wall, where the donkeys shelter in winter and where Lama used to hide in the rafters when she was wild; and opposite is the white seat with the verbena beside it where Jeannie's mother was quietly reading the paper when Fred, then a three-week-old donkey startled her by bashing his head into it. And it was on this white seat that Lama sat for the photograph that Shelagh

11

secretly took to give us a surprise present for Lama's first Christmas.

Away past the barn runs the lane which did not exist when we first came to Minack, through the little stream which is called at this point Monty's Leap after Monty of *A Cat in the Window,* then winding up the hill to the farm buildings of our neighbours at the top, then on to the Penzance road over a mile away. We cannot see the farm buildings from the bridge. We cannot see any building except a farm in the very distance on the other side of Lamorna valley. So when we stand on the bridge we gaze at wild land, except for a field or two; and at the expanse of Mount's Bay, and the sweep of the Lizard.

Between the fields behind us where the cows graze, and the field where the donkeys spend hours of their time staring down at the little garden and the porch, trying to will us to pay them attention, lies a stony stretch of land at the top of which is our well. This well, we were advised by a dowser, would gush water at fifteen feet. This depth was reached by the miners we engaged to dig it; and the soil remained dry as a desert. There was the splendid hole, so splendid that farmers would come from miles around on Sunday afternoons to have a look at it; and all our money was going down it. Twenty feet, twenty-five feet, at last at thirty feet a great shout went up from the bottom of the well: 'Water! Water!' It was still not enough and we had to drill a special hole four feet long before there was any quantity to pump to a storage tank. There is not enough even now in a dry summer. But when the main supply was brought to the farms of our neighbours, we ourselves refused to have it. The well may be inconvenient, but the freshness of the water is incomparable.

On the way up to the well, there is a small wooden gate into the donkey field. From there they can watch us on the bridge, and if they are bored they will paw at the gate, rattling it, so that we have to look. I was looking at them when I saw the swallow skimming the field behind them. And when I shouted out: 'Swallow!' to Jeannie the donkeys thought I was shouting at them, and they began to hee-haw. Fred's hee-haw is a fine trumpeting, but poor Penny groans up and down the scale as if she had never known how to hee-haw properly. There they were then, singing away in their own fashion, as Jeannie came out of the cottage to join me.

The first swallow is one of the original pleasures. Nature triumphing over man is always a pleasant act of reassurance that we have still a long, long way to go before computers rule the universe. Humans may be drilled into uniformity, but no one is going to control a bird who flies thousands of miles to Africa in the autumn, and back again in the spring to the same cave of a house, the same barn. So when I see the first swallow I rejoice because freedom still is with us.

Swallows had never nested at Minack. I supposed that the reason may have been that we were so close to the sea, or because we were almost their first landfall, or they needed to see more of the country before they decided to stop; or it may have been that the buildings just were not suitable. There had been times in other years when, for a day or two, we thought the luck had changed; and we would see a pair flying in and out of the narrow doorway of the barn, and up and around the cottage, and Jeannie would hope her wish would come true. But the swallows always failed her. They were not satisfied with the arrangements at Minack. And on they would fly.

When the swallows arrive, and the whitethroats, and the chiff chaffs and the warblers, and other migratory birds, the holiday season has begun. Robins, wrens, blue tits and coal tits, hedge sparrows and dunnocks and all the other birds who never move a mile or two from their base, find the foreigners pecking about beside them. Favourite perches at night are occupied; and nesting sites. And a branch which a robin thought was his own is now the branch whence a flycatcher from Morocco dashes on his short-lived expeditions. This is the beginning of a period of justifiable upset among the local inhabitants. Cornwall is under occupation in woods, gardens, shore and towns. But the donkeys, within the restriction of their own standards, are at peace. Holidaymakers will be coming to flatter them. Cameras will be pointing at them. Rides will be asked for by shy children. The summer is their time.

13

We watched the first swallow soar and swoop over the wood for a minute or two, then on it flew towards Lamorna valley. Others would be following but the first, it is always the first, that one remembers. It meant the prospect of summer, and the coming of unexpected adventures, and the gentle illusion that we were as young as we always had been. We stood silently on the bridge. This was one of its pleasures that we could sit or stand there, gazing our lives away. There were so many small incidents taking place that were of great importance to ourselves, but would not appear important to those who have to drive themselves to pursue conventional values. Why waste time observing a fox, the same fox you saw yesterday and the day before, nosing about looking for mice? Why be surprised again at the way the rabbits sit on their hind legs like a dog doing a begging trick, watching the fox at a distance? Why not bolt for a hole? Why does the fox if he is looking for food pass them by, except for token attacks? What was that wild cry? A water rail? There is a green woodpecker rapping at the trunk of an elm in the wood. Which one? And are the blue tits nesting in the box we nailed to the tree by the camellia? The willow tree is greening. I'm glad the flowers of the cherry tree have not been spoilt by a gale this year. The Scillonian is late, isn't she? She's coming round the point now. The Stephensons' fishing fleet went out this morning so the weather will be staying fine. What glorious colours the French paint their crabbers . . . look at the brilliant green of that one. I saw her last week in Newlyn harbour. Someone is coming down the lane. No, false alarm. Get the glasses, quick, there's something moving in the corner of Bill's field . . . oh, it's only his dachshund. Bill was one of the farmers at the top of the hill.

When we stood on the bridge we did not see the path because of the escallonia. We could see Boris or Lama begin to walk up the path, then they disappeared behind the escallonia, and we heard them instead. Lama was a little cat but the noise of her paws on the grey chippings as she came towards us was loud enough for Jeannie to joke sometimes: 'An elephant is coming.' And the elephant would appear beside us, collapsing on the grey chippings, turning on her back, inviting us to bend down and stroke a greeting. Boris never came to the bridge. We would listen to his plod, plod, plod on the chippings, then he would turn right instead of left and would waddle his way to the door of the porch where he would wait for one of us to attend to him.

We used to ask people who we thought might be knowledgeable if they had any idea how long muscovy drakes lived; and some would answer they didn't know because the only muscovy drakes they had possessed went sooner than later into the pot; and others gave us the answer we wanted to hear, that muscovy drakes were long living birds. 'I remember one when I was a boy,' said a bird fancier whose views were particularly welcome, 'which flew over our farmhouse when he was sixteen.'

Jane had brought Boris to us eight years before, and we didn't know how old he was then. She appeared one morning with Boris in her arms, having carried him across the fields from the cottage in which she lived overlooking the cliffs a half mile away. A young farmer had given him to her in a mistaken gesture of courtship. He had arrived at her door with a sack, and explained he had brought her a good dinner. Thereupon Jane opened the sack, saw the muscovy drake inside, and burst into tears. She kept Boris for a couple of days in her bedroom until her mother decided it was not a suitable place; and so she brought him to Minack. I remember I did not want him. I did not want the responsibility of looking after such a bird. I was devoting all my attention at the time to maintaining the existence of the flower farm, and I did not want my interest diverted by the problems which might come with a muscovy drake. Might he not fly round the district, resulting in hours of wasted time searching for him? And would he be content to remain a bachelor? I raised these points and nobody listened. Jane, Shelagh and Jeannie just went on with their work, quite aware that I would soon surrender, just as I had surrendered a few months before when Lama had first come on the scene.

He was christened Boris after Boris Pasternak. There was a boy that summer staying nearby on holiday called Julius, and he would come over every day and spend it with us and Jane and Shelagh. Sometimes he would arrive before

15

breakfast as we were cutting the lettuces for the Penzance market; and he would arrive full of the pleasure he had had from his walk along the cliff and across the fields where he was staying. He was sensitive and erudite for his age, and he was an admirer of both Dr Zhivago and Boris Pasternak's poetry. He it was who decided that Boris should be called Boris; and he it was who dug the hole where we placed an old galvanised bath. I remember filling it with water, then hopefully waiting for Boris to take his first swim, waiting discreetly at a distance along with Julius; and then the shout of Julius: 'He's in it!' Boris, as happens with such birds and animals, was not just loved by us for himself. He was a link with a past which we often like to remember. A year after that first bathe in the galvanised bath Julius was killed in a motor accident; and a year later Shelagh died.

Boris had become slower in his movements, and that was the reason why we had begun to worry a little about him. He no longer perched on the wooden bar, a couple of feet from the floor, in the chicken house at night. The effort of reaching it seemed too much for him, and so he squatted in a corner instead; and during the day he squatted more than he used to do in the various places of his territory he occupied. There was a lichen covered rock he passed to and from the chicken house which was a favourite place of his; and we could see this rock from the bridge. We had now built a small cement based pool for him in front of the shed where Geoffrey sits at lunchtimes; and after his bathe, after flapping his wings in the pool so that the water was in turmoil, he would plod to the rock and dry himself. He would flap his white wings again, and there was a sound in the air as if a carpet was being beaten; and then for a while he would stand on the rock with his wings a little apart from his body so that the breeze could dry his feathers. When he believed himself dry, he would waggle his beautiful green black tail feathers, tuck his head and yellow beak inside a wing, and go to sleep. And if he wasn't on the rock he might be by the old stone wall which faces the sun and which was also a favourite dozing place of Lama's And the two of them would be there, side by side. There were other places he would like to go, and they were all close to the cottage. So we were startled when, one afternoon that April, we found he was in none of them.

'Perhaps he has gone to bed early,' I said. And I went down to the chicken house and found it empty. At that moment I began to feel afraid.

When Boris first came to us, indeed for years afterwards, we were blind to the possibility of foxes attacking him. We, of course, locked him up at night, but during the day, despite the fact we would often watch a fox roaming the field on the other side of the shallow valley, we never considered he was in danger. Then a neighbour said he was astonished at our foolishness. 'Do you mean you let him wander about when you are out?' he asked in amazement. And from then on we were always on guard.

But on this particular April day we had left him on his own. We had taken the car to Sennen and walked along the beach, and when we returned, Geoffrey had already gone home. Lama was waiting for us by the door and we let her in, and Jeannie filled her plate with a spoonful of fish. The donkeys were peering down at us from the field, and so I took a couple of chocolate biscuits to them, and stayed a minute or two beside them as they munched. Then I went down below the cottage and found Boris missing.

We both panicked. We rushed hither and thither calling for him at the top of our voices, hysterical behaviour which was to be funny in retrospect. After ten minutes we were no longer looking for a live Boris, and were searching instead for a trace of his feathers. I ran through the wood with my eyes on the ground, then back across the donkey field, past the cottage and down the lane. I felt enraged with myself for being so careless, and sickened at the thought that Boris should end his days as a meal for cubs.

And then suddenly I saw him.

I had dashed into the field where we have our mobile greenhouses, still scanning the ground for feathers, when I became aware of a white blob at the far end. I went racing across the field shouting: 'Boris! Boris! What the hell have you been up to?' He had never strayed so far in his life, and when I reached him he was quite unperturbed, and he

17

looked at me as if he was asking what all the fuss was about. Perhaps he was thinking he had played a funny joke on us. Perhaps it was his way of telling us that it was foolish to worry about his well-being. He would still, at the age of sixteen, fly over Minack.

Nor was Lama a wanderer. Indeed I have never seen her except on Minack land though once, when she was a wild kitten, she was seen by a neighbour in the old quarry which bordered the land we once rented. This was less than a year after Monty had died, the cat who had come with us from London; and on the day he died I had sworn that I would never have another cat unless a black cat whose home was unknown came to our door in a storm. I said this to Jeannie because I had been an anti-cat man before Monty had come into my life; and though he himself had won my heart, I did not believe that any other cat would win me again. But I had always been superstitious about black cats. And so some spirit within me moved me to make this stipulation which I naturally never expected to be fulfilled.

Lama, after roaming our meadows for a month before-hand, did in fact come miaowing to the door in a storm. And there was nobody in the area who had lost her. And she *was* quite black except for a wisp of white on her shirt front.

So where had she come from? Jeannie's firm opinion is that she was born in a little cave down the cliff. The clues are these.

For a time before Lama was first seen in our meadows, we had observed a small grey Persian cat passing occasionally within sight of the cottage. There was no question of it ever wishing to be friendly, and it ran away if we ever came too near. And after Lama at last chose to come in from the wild, and become a normal, home-loving cat, we continued to see the grey Persian at intervals in the distance.

We did not for a moment associate her with Lama, and we would never have done so had we not had the strange experience of finding another black kitten, the replica of Lama, six years after Lama had come to us.

This second black kitten was discovered by Jeannie curled up asleep in a little cave down the cliff. For a few

18

days afterwards, Geoffrey and I and another man who was helping us to plant bulbs would catch a glimpse of it in the undergrowth, darting about like a wild rabbit. We had already noticed that the grey Persian was regularly in our neighbourhood, and now we observed it repeatedly coming up and down the cliff when it thought we were not watching.

Then one evening as dusk was falling we found the grey Persian crouched on the branch of an elm near the cottage ... and a couple of feet away on the same branch was Lama. We had never, of course, seen them together before, and we could not help but notice that they were the same shape and size. And what was so puzzling was the way they were treating each other. They appeared to be so deep in conversation that they were unaware that we were watching them. Guess as you please what subject they were communing about. All I can tell you is that the next morning I found the black kitten curled up on a sack in the barn.

During its stay we used to watch it through a window on the lane side of the barn. Shy as ever, it spent most of its time hidden from sight amongst the paraphernalia of fertiliser bags and various implements; and only when Jeannie had placed a saucer of bread and milk on the cobbled stone floor were we able to see it. Then it would creep from its hide-out, crouch by the saucer and nervously lap. There was no doubt about its similarity to Lama. Indeed it was the exact double of Lama when she was a wild black kitten.

It was now that Jeannie christened the grey Persian Daisy. Jeannie was convinced that the grey Persian was the mother of the black kitten as well as the mother of Lama, and so she merited a name. Why Daisy I don't know. I think Jeannie thought the name gave an idea of what the grey Persian, and her brood, looked like. But once the kitten had disappeared we did not see Daisy again for several months.

Such an absence had happened before. It still does. So many weeks go by without us seeing her that we come to the conclusion she must be dead ... and then she reappears. One of us may suddenly find her down the cliff, or Geoffrey will call to us that he has just seen her in the donkey field, or we will be on the bridge and catch sight of her slowly

19

following the route she has always followed when she passes through Minack. She comes through the greenhouse field, over the hedge and into the lane, down the lane towards the cottage and across Monty's Leap by a wooden plank, then she turns left over the bank into the stable field where the Cromwell daffodils have been left undisturbed for thirty years and more, across this field to a foot wide track which badgers have padded for centuries, then on to the top of the cemetery field where she either takes the path to the cliff, or goes right towards what we call the onion meadow, past the meadow where I first saw Lama, staring at me, assessing me, from beds of calendula. Her return journey does not always follow the same route. She chooses instead, to be surprised by Jeannie passing the washing line. The line is beside the well above the cottage. Wherever she is, she will never permit us to come too close.

You have a good view of the stable field from the bridge. I was standing there one afternoon when I saw Daisy again after an interval of two or three months. She was following the route I have described, exactly the same route that she was following before Lama came into our lives. But instead of being excited at seeing her again after such an interval, I was annoyed that she was there at all. She was distracting me. My purpose of standing on the bridge was to watch a pair of swallows whose behaviour promised that at last Jeannie and I would have the pleasure of saying that swallows nested at Minack. They had been flying in and out of the barn for the previous few days and now, at the very moment I should have been exclaiming to Jeannie that I had seen Daisy again, I had observed the swallows swoop down to Monty's Leap, settle for a few seconds beside the stream, then dip their beaks in the shallow mud bordering it . . . and a moment later fly back to the barn, diving at speed through the narrow doorway. A minute passed, and out they came again, down to the stream, beaks into the mud, then in a flash into the barn.

No wonder I wasn't interested in Daisy.

For the first time since we came here, swallows had chosen to spend the summer at Minack.

20

THREE

There was another cottage in our lives before Minack. We found it one summer day when we were taking the Poljigga road towards Land's End, the road which runs out of Penzance by the promenade, across Newlyn Bridge, then up steep Paul Hill, winding its way a couple of miles distant from the coast, past the curiously named village of Sheffield and up Boleigh Hill past Lamorna turn on the left, and on past Boskenna then Treverven Farm and Sparnon, down and up the beautiful valley of Penberth, past Treen, then Poljigga and a mile or two later joining the A30 for the last stretch to Land's End.

We were on holiday; Jeannie from her job as Press

Officer of the Savoy, Claridges and Berkeley; and myself from my job as a member of MI5.

We had no purpose in mind except to roam the countryside, pausing now and again, discovering a part of Cornwall that neither of us knew. In a way I am wrong to say that I did not know it. When I was a small boy spending holidays at my home of Glendorgal near Newquay, I always felt a mystical attraction for these far west lands of Cornwall; and presumably this attraction was developed by fleeting expeditions, picnics with aunts and uncles crammed in some ancient car, great voyages across the wastes of Camborne and Redruth, to St Ives and Zennor and Land's End. I do not remember any details, just a vague sense of adventure, though there is one such adventure I remember clearly.

My father's old friend was the Chief Constable of Cornwall at the time when my brothers and I were children; and every year he gave us a treat which lifted us into a sphere of great importance. He was a precise man, a bachelor, and he fought at Omdurman with Churchill; and as a child I never tired of his telling the story of that battle over and over again. He was a fascinating story teller, quiet voice, quiet humour; and as Chief Constable he was looked upon as a father figure by his men. He knew each member of his force individually, took a personal interest in their families. From the moment I first remember him, he suffered from imaginary ill health; he died peacefully when he was eighty-six.

His official car was a Sunbeam, an open tourer, and he would arrive in it, driven by a chauffeur in police uniform punctually at eleven o'clock on the chosen morning. Our host would sit in the front, and my two brothers and myself in the back with our feet making room for the inviting looking hamper on the floor. The hamper, of course, gave us a pleasant sense of anticipation, so too did the moment when the luxurious vehicle glided away up Glendorgal drive, my mother and father waving us goodbye, and set off for Land's End. But the real excitement, stimulated by our childish vanity, was the knowledge that our host had organised a surprise which was not in fact a surprise. The Chief Constable, we secretly knew, had arranged that every village constable on the route, every inspector, sergeant and constable that could be spared in the towns of Redruth, Camborne and Hayle and Penzance, were waiting for us at strategic points; and as the Sunbeam hove into sight they jumped smartly to attention and saluted as we passed. We took their salutes as if they were our due.

I loved my home of Glendorgal. There was an occasion when I was at Harrow that I startled my fellow Harrovians by preferring to go there instead of attending the then great social occasion of the Eton and Harrow match at Lord's. The night train to Cornwall, just two days there then the night train back? Quite mad. Missing two days of strutting round Lord's in the finery of morning coat and elegant trousers and double-breasted grey waistcoat, cornflower in buttonhole? Extraordinary.

But Glendorgal was the most beautiful place in the world for me. This low, granite house with fat granite chimneys, now made famous as a hotel by my brother Nigel, lay snug beside its own private cove with views of rugged loveliness up the coast to Trevose Head in the far distance. The grounds were of wild Cornish moorland dropping cliffs into the sea, and here I used to hunt rabbits and to play with Bruce, a white, long-coated mongrel, and Lance my old English sheepdog, and Roy his successor. Here, too, aged six, I once started to dig to Australia because I had been told that the continent lay at the other side of the earth. My father had a fierce passion for Glendorgal. I have seen him by the hour standing by the sundial which is still there, gazing at the sea and the island opposite, and wandering around the grounds puffing his pipe; and when he went away on some business he would return in two days when others might have been away for three; and when we three boys began to bring girls to stay at Glendorgal we used to warn them that if they were to be liked by my father they must tell him how beautiful they thought it was. If they didn't feel as he did, we would have been aware that they had not been accepted. Such a situation never arose. It seemed impossible for anyone to be cool about the rugged loveliness of Glendorgal.

Jeannie never stayed there. When she came into my life,

my father had been forced financially to rent Glendorgal, and he and my mother were living in a cottage called Cavern Cottage on the other side of the bay from where my father used to look endlessly at our old home through a telescope. 'Every inch, every pebble, every blade of grass,' I heard him once say to himself as he stared through his telescope, 'I know intimately . . . and a damned stranger has to live there.' He was then a Deputy Lieutenant of Cornwall, Chairman of the Quarter Sessions, and Commandant of the Special Constabulary. It was war time, and he was also organising on behalf of Stuart Menzies, late head of MI6, a network of agents, wireless experts and couriers in Cornwall, who were to go into operation should the Germans invade and occupy the southwest. My father was, in fact, an unpaid public servant.

He had already sold the island opposite Glendorgal; and his way of doing so made certain that this island belonged to those who loved taste, rather than convenience, for all time to come. Newquay council had begun to negotiate for the island, connected to the mainland by a fifty-foot footbridge, before the time of compulsory purchase, before the National Trust had become the vogue. My father needed money, not for any extravagances on his part, but because he wanted to maintain Glendorgal, and my mother, and perhaps give some future to his sons. The council offered a good price, for they foresaw that this area of the Newquay environment had a huge holiday future, and my father was about to accept. Then suddenly, as he sat at his big Victorian desk which my brother Nigel still uses, he realised what would happen. He knew that Cornish councils tended to build public lavatories on beautiful sites; small ugly buildings, breeze block and cemented, which gave councillors a great sense of pride. He suddenly imagined such a building perched on the island where mounds of ancient burial grounds had hitherto reigned supreme. He thereupon demanded that in any conditions of sale no public lavatory should be built on the island; and the council agreed and took a thousand pounds off the price, and the skyline was preserved for ever. If you ever go to this island, you will find a granite seat with my father's name on it, and which my mother put there in his memory. It faces Glendorgal.

Jeannie, therefore, was never part of my home when we lived there, but she had a bond with my father, and when we became engaged my father gave us dinner the same evening at a restaurant called the Good Intent in the Kings Road in Chelsea. We sat at a corner table and he drank our toast and wished us well; and within a year he had died. But at this dinner he was telling Jeannie that there was only one other home in Cornwall which he considered compared to Glendorgal; and this was Boskenna. The Boskenna which was on the Poljigga road to Land's End. There we were a few years later driving past it.

I had no intention of stopping, indeed, I was not even sure that it was the place concerned. Cornwall is full of huge estates with mysterious drives to great houses you cannot see from the road; and there was no sign to show that this was Boskenna. Two huge stone pillars acted as sentries to the drive, and there were the usual woods, and the usual question mark as to where lay the house. We went on, the woods sprawling the landscape towards the sea, following the road which dipped into a valley then up again past a farmhouse with a thatched roof.

Jeannie said suddenly: 'I'm quite sure your father is telling us to stop. I mean it . . . that *was* Boskenna we passed, and we *must* turn back.'

I respect Jeannie's intuition. Indeed we both find it wiser for us to follow our intuition than it is for us to follow reason. Reason, with all its pros and cons, its good sense and caution, makes us woolly minded and negative. Intuition, on the other hand, has led us again and again to behave irrationally, providing us with the chance to achieve the impossible. Jeannie's intuition at that moment, for instance, changed the course of our lives.

I turned back; and intuition guided us again. We might normally have made a call at Boskenna, if it was Boskenna. My father had been a friend of the owner, and my mother used to recount that at dinner parties he would flirt with her. His name was Colonel Paynter, a relic of this country's feudal past, a landowner who had a paternal interest in

25

those who worked for him, believing that their welfare was his duty, and not that of the Government. His attitude seemed praiseworthy at the time, and so it was within its narrow sphere. He benevolently ruled the district, giving a sense of permanent security to all his subjects. His word was law, his favours came from heaven. The first time we met him, he took us to a meadow where men and women were lifting new potatoes. It was a hot June afternoon; and the Colonel, small and bent, leaning on a walking stick and incongruously wearing a bowler hat, his pockets bulging with apples, shuffled round to each person, handing out an apple as if it was a golden coin. It was received as such.

But that day I turned back we did not call at Boskenna. I stopped the car instead by a gate in the valley below the farmhouse with the thatched roof. The gate is still there, on the coast side of the road, and it is painted white now. The path we then followed was only a foot wide, and it ran through the woods beside the stream until it passed two cottages, then it dipped towards the stream which was crossed by stepping stones on up the other side until it faded away from the woods into a small field which edged the sea. I remember we hastened along this path as if we had an urgent mission to perform, an appointment to keep; and as we reached the small field, marvelling at the gentle swell of the sea which was sparkling a bay guarded by boulders, not by cliffs, we suddenly saw St en Dellon.

It was an old cottage in so isolated a position, in a setting seemingly so perfect, that it is understandable that we both jumped to the conclusion that it was our dream cottage. How could we know at that moment that it was an illusion, that we were in fact seeing Minack?

For until we saw St en Dellon we had never considered the prospect of having a cottage in Cornwall. We had never thought of leaving London and uprooting ourselves from the life we were leading. But the sight of St en Dellon on that summer's day brought another dimension into our lives, and we knew we could never be the same again.

We had no chance of acquiring St en Dellon from the beginning, but this did not stop us from imagining that we

26

could do so. And we took courage from the attitude of the old couple who lived there. They told us that they did not like the cottage because it was so lonely, and that they would prefer to live in the village. This sounded most promising. We visited them a second time and the old man, thick white hair and a face like Popeye the Sailor, told us that the sooner he could leave the better. We listened attentively, made sympathetic noises, and believed every word he said. There was a small boy, some relation, living at the cottage too, dark and sturdy like the true Cornishman, and he used to stare at us silently as we talked. On our third visit I thought I caught sight of him disappearing up a path as we approached the cottage. We had another pleasant conversation with the old couple, and as by this time we had met the Colonel (he owned St en Dellon), I explained that I was trying to persuade him to offer them one of the estate cottages in the village. They nodded politely but their manner on this occasion gave me the uncomfortable feeling that all the time they had been humouring us . . . the old Cornish way of agreeing with all that an up country visitor has to say and only telling him what he wishes to hear. There was still no sign of the boy when we said good-bye, and set off back to the car. There it was as I left it by the gate . . . except for the tyres. They were flat. The valves of all four had been loosened.

We were undaunted. Nor were we put off by the lack of decisiveness on the part of the Colonel. He appeared to be helping us yet there was no positive sign that he was actually doing so. He was intrigued, however, by Jeannie and the setting in which she lived and worked; and this we thought might be in our favour. This was the world in which he used to move many, many years before; and he used to question her about people long since dead. He asked for the gossip about them. He seemed not to realise that he had been left behind. And after our holiday and we were back in London, he would still write and ask for news. Like the old couple at St en Dellon, he was humouring us along. Like them, he had no intention of furthering our ambitions. Might we not be as lightweight as others from a city who came to Cornwall gushing their wish to be away from it all?

He had seen them many times before. All froth and excitement as they upset some standing situation. Then grumbles and disenchantment, and away . . . leaving another failure for the local people to remember.

The following May we returned to continue our campaign, and we stayed at Lamorna, three miles down the coast. We did not know that we were close to Minack. We did not know as we set out that first morning of our holiday to walk along the cliffs to St en Dellon that we were indeed about to see the cottage of our dreams.

We had reached a high point of the cliffs, and had sat down on a rock, the sea surging far below us, the sweep of the Lizard peninsula to our left, the rugged coast running away towards Porthcurno and Gwennap Head on our right, the land behind us a jungle of yellow gorse and young green bracken and savage brambles; and while we sat there, the soft sea air on our faces, we saw a buzzard gliding high in the sky above us. It began to drift inland, and as we watched its motionless wings, marvelling at the way they effortlessly made use of the eddies in the atmosphere, we suddenly saw below it in the distance, a small grey cottage on the edge of a wood. It was as grey as the boulders heaped haphazardly in the land around it, as grey as the ancient stone hedges which guarded long forgotten meadows. This was Minack. We knew at the instant of seeing it that it was to become our home.

We now no longer courted the Colonel. A prominent farmer in the district took his place, and months of more frustrating negotiations then followed. It was more than a year later that we saw the Colonel for the last time. We were outside the Lamorna telephone box and we had at last been told that we could rent the cottage of Minack and the land around it. He peered through the window of his old car, bowler hat perched on his head, and looked quizzically at Jeannie for a moment. Then he enquired:

'And is the casket worthy of the jewel?'

FOUR

Minack had no water or electricity when we first came to
live here. The land was a wilderness, there was no lane for
cars, the living room had earth for its floor. Neighbours
were sure we would be back in London within six months.
Jeannie, they said, could not possibly stick it. She might
tolerate the summer but the winter never. Yet she was not
to mind cooking meals on a primus stove, or lighting paraffin lamps with a wick soaked in methylated spirits. Primitive living, as others find, is the perfect antidote to over
sophistication. There was space in the sky, and time was
ours, and the air we breathed came to us from far away
across the sea, and we listened to birds singing which we

29

hadn't noticed before, and we were able to watch them without having to hurry forward to heaven knows where. There were no conventions to obey, and all we wanted was to live the same kind of life as the crofters who once lived at Minack. Such a halcyon situation was hardly likely to last.

We had to earn a living out of the wilderness of land, and before this could happen we had to reclaim meadows which for years had been neglected. And then we had to begin to pay for our mistakes. We had only our enthusiasm to teach us and time and again this enthusiasm went very much astray. Nor could these mistakes be quickly corrected. A crop had to fail several times, due to the permutation of causes for its failure, before we could finally decide to discard it. Thus we grew massive amounts of potatoes for several seasons in succession before we were convinced they were uneconomical. This happened also with violets, wallflowers, calendulas, forget-me-nots, stocks and even with freesias; for there came a time when we invested in greenhouses and we were sure that freesias would be the ideal winter crop, and it was, until so many other people had the same idea that the market became glutted. We have reached the stage now when we only grow tomatoes and daffodils; and the daffodils in the spring of this year I am writing about gave us the best harvest we had ever known since we came to Minack.

So on the sunny April morning after we had loaded the last of the daffodils into the flower train at Penzance station, we celebrated by taking the winding path down the cliff to the rocks and the sea below. We had brought in a basket beef sandwiches of home-made bread, a couple of wine glasses, a corkscrew, and a bottle of *Côtes du Rhône*. It was one of those pleasant moments when one could look back on past efforts with calm detachment. The daffodil harvest is the foundation upon which we can plan the year; and now we could foresee a summer without financial concern.

Daffodil seasons are seldom orderly. The aim of a daffodil grower is to spread the harvest over several weeks, and so he stocks his flower farm with bulb varieties that follow each other in sequence.

In our case we begin with the deep yellow trumpet called Magnificence which professionals call Mags, and follow on with another golden yellow called Golden Harvest. Then comes a miniature King Alfred with the ugly name of Oblivaris but exquisite to look at and wonderfully long-lasting once picked; then a lovely large yellow trumpet called Joseph McLeod; then a variety with two names, California or Pentewan, a bright yellow cupped narcissi with a sweet scent and which thrives on our land; then a few Rembrandt, and a charming daffodil with the atrocious name of Sulphur which we now call Lamorna because it fetches a better price by so doing; and then the whites . . . Early Bride, Brunswick, Barrett Browning (a beautiful creamy-white perianth with a brilliant red cup), White Lion and Actaea. Actaea is a prolific cropper with a large pure white perianth, a brilliant scarlet eye and an exquisite scent; and when the last box of these has been sent away to Covent Garden, our harvest is over.

This may appear to be a simple sequence of events, a kind of factory conveyor belt which needs only the efficiency of man to turn out the goods required. Factories, however, can slow down output when the shelves are full, or increase it when they are emptying, whereas daffodil growers are at the mercy of the weather. Too warm a spring and all the varieties come rushing in together; too cold a one and they are held back, thus producing a glut as soon as the weather changes.

Such an untidy situation has attracted the attention of the planners who sit in their Whitehall offices, anxious to help the men of the soil; and I once attended a conference where a gentleman from Whitehall explained what should be done about the matter. Among his audience were some of the largest growers of daffodils in both Cornwall and the Isles of Scilly, and they were at the time being confronted (it was one of the warm springs) with acres of daffodils without the time and labour to pick them. The neatly dressed fellow talked to us as if God had no hand in the affair. 'You should have planned your varieties more carefully,' said he. 'You should hold the blooms back so that they do not flood the market . . . you should co-operate.' And so on. There we were puffing at our pipes, gaping at the fellow, while the sun was blazing and the nights were as warm as those of mid summer.

Yet there were some growers, in the Lincolnshire bulb area for instance, who listened to such advice, and they began holding back their surplus blooms in the refrigeration plants (pre-cooled bulbs produce, of course, earlier blooms). Then when they thought the market was more favourable, they took them out of the refrigerators and despatched them. Unfortunately they had not foreseen the effect of the refrigeration on the daffodils. The florists soon told them. 'Your daffodils melt,' came the cry, 'as soon as we unpack them.' One, therefore, prays for a spring when the weather is persistently cool, a steady even temperature which neither forces a variety or holds it back so that it clashes with another; and this is what happened this time.

It was one of those years, too, when every bulb seemed to produce a flower, and that is by no means a usual experience. Many a time I have walked the daffodil meadows a week or two before the season would normally begin and observed with dismay that few buds were showing, that the bulbs had only thrown up foliage. Some varieties are more temperamental than others, and one of these is the golden trumpet Magnificence. More often than not we have dolefully said to each other: 'The Mags are going to be light this year.' There they would be in lush rows of green foliage, and hardly a flower to be seen. I had bought them in the first place as the result of listening to the advice of an old man in the pub at Treen not far away. He told me, as he downed his pints, such heart warming stories of the money he had made from his Magnificence that Jeannie and I forthwith decided to follow suit. It was one of our failings, when we first came to Minack, that we listened too readily to those who set out to please us. We wanted to be assured that prosperity lay ahead of us, and so wise old men were good-natured enough to tell us what we wanted to believe.

Yet I have to admit that much of the failure to produce bulbs that flower regularly was due to our method of cultivation. We have to be old-fashioned in our methods because the contours of the land prevent us from being otherwise. The stretch of coast between Penzance and Gwennap Head used to provide those first early daffodils from the mainland which set the heart and the soul alight when you suddenly saw them for sale in mid January. Those were the true daffodils, and still are when you find them in the shops. They are grown in small pocket meadows, high hedges attempting to protect them from the salt of the gales, and the warm climate hastening their blooming. They demanded, however, much attention. Every stage of cultivation, for instance, was done by hand. When in the summer the daffodil foliage had died down, the bulbs every three years were hacked, though with great care, out of the ground and laid in rows to dry; and later they were picked up, put into bags and taken to the steam sterilisation plant for a three hour sterilising period . . . sterilisation of bulb fly and eel worm which are the scourge of daffodils. And when that was done, the bulbs were not returned to the same meadows. Early potatoes would in due course fill their meadows, while the bulbs filled the potato meadows. And all the work was done by hand.

But the price obtained for these very early daffodils – perhaps three or four shillings a bunch less commission and cost of freight – made the work worth while; and a daffodil grower was indeed foolish if he didn't look after his bulbs. Unfortunately for us cliff growers, stories of the prices we obtained tempted others to discover methods that enabled them to compete with us. The method of pre-cooled bulbs grown in greenhouses, resulted in the market being swamped by factory grown daffodils, weeks, even months before the true, naturally grown daffodil of the cliffs was ready to be picked. And inevitably the price dropped so that today we have to be satisfied when we receive a shilling a bunch.

This competition, and the regular increase in expenses, make it economically impossible to look after the cliff bulbs. The big growers, on the other hand, can use sophisticated machines in their large fields, machines which can lift two acres of bulbs a day; machines which sort out the sizes of bulbs, machines which can replant the bulbs at great speed;

all the paraphernalia, in fact, that comes with big business in any sphere. Such treatment guarantees that most of their bulbs will flower every year.

We, on the other hand, have to leave our cliff bulbs virtually untouched, just a very few being lifted in a year; and thus some of them have been lying in the ground undisturbed for ten years and more. Indeed, according to the experts, it is a miracle that the bulbs are still there at all. Disease, bulb fly and eel worm, should have decimated them. But many still thrive, the foliage in any case. And this year, the year of our success, they all flowered. No one could explain what had provoked them to do this.

The Mags, even the Mags were in profusion. The Oblivaris or Obs as we call them, which had lain in meadows long before we took them over, which had never before shown a bud, these too came bursting into flower. And there were blooms in all the hedges, and they came from bulbs which had been tossed there during the war when bulb ground had been required for potatoes, and the order had been made that the bulbs should be thrown away. There they were, Scilly Whites, Obs, Buxton and other old varieties which I did not recognise. Over twenty years later and they were still ready to bloom.

Apart from this bonanza of flowers, apart from the amiable weather, there were other reasons for the best season ever. Up to recently the market, and the public, wanted to buy daffodils only when they were in full bloom. We had to gear all our sendings to suit these requirements, providing ourselves with a vast amount of extra work, and doing harm to the daffodils in the process. We had to have a heat room, for instance, separate from the shed where we bunched because, with daffodils being picked in great numbers there could not possibly be enough room in the shed to allow them to come out naturally. Nor could they be left in the meadows because of the threat of wind damage. Hence the method had to be used by growers of forcing them into full bloom by putting them overnight in a room so heated by paraffin stoves that the water in the galvanised pails next morning was warm.

But all this belongs to the past; and we have largely to

thank the Dutch for the change. The Dutch are not interested in marketing daffodils in this country, but they are interested in exporting ever increasing quantities of bulbs. Thus the leaders of their bulb industry came to the conclusion that they themselves were being harmed by our traditional methods of marketing daffodils; and that sooner or later the public would turn against buying daffodils which in turn would affect the sale of their bulbs. Thereupon they decided to launch an advertising campaign in this country to persuade the public to buy daffodils in bud.

The success of the campaign has not only meant you can buy a bunch of daffodils which will last twice as long in your home. It has also produced splendid benefits to growers like ourselves. Our work is done more quickly. Picking, for instance, is easier. We don't have to worry so much about gales because the daffodil is now picked as soon as the head has dropped, the calex is broken and the yellow of the bud is showing. Nor is there the tedious task of filling the heat room with galvanised pails, then transferring them laboriously to the packing shed in the morning. Bunching is quicker as well. Since, in the old days, every bloom of a bunch had to be wide open, it often meant searching the pails for them, temporarily discarding the flowers which were not fully open. Packing, too, is easier, and more economical. We used to pack fifteen bunches in a box; now, because buds don't take up so much room, we can pack thirty bunches in the same size of box; and so money is saved on boxes and money is saved on freight.

But there still remains the problem of warm weather. At the beginning of the season, in January and February, picking in bud can be kept under control. In March, however, when it is warm and the bulk of the crop is maturing, control is impossible, and the meadows become a mass of open daffodils. At least they have not been forced in a heat room.

Therefore, remember this about early daffodils. The old-fashioned, Cornish grown, unforced early daffodil will never appear in the shops until the middle of January . . . except the heavenly scented narcissus Sol d'Or which comes from November onwards from the Isles of Scilly. Mqst of those others you see are artificially grown in vast hangars of greenhouses. Would Wordsworth have written a poem about such daffodils?

So there we were, Jeannie and I, the daffodil season behind us, on our way down the path to Minack rocks. The gulls rose in usual annoyance into the sky, wheeling and crying, leaving a cormorant silhouetted for a moment on the pointed rock where sometimes I fish for pollack; and then it too flapped its wings, and flew away low over the sea towards Lamorna Cove. We reached the flat rock where we had decided to picnic, and the sun warmed us as I brought out the bottle of wine from the basket, and Jeannie unwrapped the sandwiches.

'Do you realise,' she said, as I was opening the bottle, that this is the first summer since we came here that we have a chance of living in the present?'

I am one of those, as it happens, who find it difficult to live in the present. I am inclined to worry about some incident in the immediate past or to anticipate some gloomy situation which I imagine may materialise in the future.

'Sounds pleasant,' I said, my mind upon the two glasses balanced unevenly on a ledge of rock and the wine I was tipping into them.

It is not an easy age for peace of mind. The dull and unimaginative can achieve a version of it, as too those young enough who still believe that youth is everlasting, so too can those who are ruthlessly ambitious, so too the men and women who are so busy organising other people's lives that they forget to organise their own. All these have peace of mind of a kind. They do not suffer the pain of self questioning and remorse. They are certain that their standards are the right standards. They are normal.

But the rest of us, those of us who have to endure the doubts and personal complexities imposed by our imaginations, are labelled maladjusted and insecure, inferior beings in fact. It is curious how the phrase that he or she is 'insecure' has become a phrase that means a bad mark. As for myself I do not understand how any human being can feel

36

secure in the modern sense of the word unless he is unbearably conceited. Philosophy, after all, is based on the premise that those who are trying to find the truth about themselves, have a sense of insecurity. Aristotle, Tagore, de Keyserling, any philosopher throughout the ages indeed, would have had no place in history if present values existed in their time. Contemplation was the motive power of their faith, periods of loneliness developed the truth of their wisdom. I wonder in what category an appointments bureau would place them if they were living today. Is there any doubt that they would be considered maladjusted and insecure?

One therefore has to try and find out about oneself against the wishes of convention. Convention needs to pump knowledge into you, not wisdom. Convention, in order to preserve what it represents, must act in the manner of a dictatorship, forcing each person to follow patterns of behaviour which, however distasteful to him, however ugly, results in the end with the declaration: 'I've got used to it.' The most repeated, the most despairing phrase of this period of the twentieth century.

When I was a schoolboy, at other times of my life too, I have sometimes felt the need to be accepted in some conventional circle whose members seemed to accept each other for granted. But such acceptance can never take place. I have felt all my life that members of a group, however worthy their intentions, are running away from themselves. I believe one has to learn to face oneself alone, to try to come to terms with all the opposites inside oneself. Groups, it seems to me, exist to blur their members from the truth, becoming mutual admiration societies except when jealousy begins to irritate. Groups, in my mind, have always mirrored escapism, not the individual who travels alone.

When Jeannie said that this was the first summer since we came to Minack that we could live in the present, my instinct was to reject her belief. I could not see myself being separated from the personal conflict which is part of me. A wonderful daffodil season, a new book to be published in the autumn, the same book to be serialised during the summer . . . these are the sort of pleasures which should have made me feel secure. I should have quickly been able to react to Jeannie's gay suggestion by saying yes. But I didn't.

I was still involved in the struggle which had brought us to this stage in our lives. I was suspicious about my ability to relax.

FIVE

When disgruntled people in cities march to meetings on May Day holding high their banners of protest, the white flowers of the blackthorn lie in drifts in Mincak woods and along the shallow valley which slopes towards the sea.

Chunky patches of golden gorse line the lane to the farm at the top of the hill, blue periwinkle spatter the banks; late primroses, wild violets, and early pink campion shelter amidst the growing grass. Fields of our neighbours where they have sown spring corn are covered by a film of green; white blossom clusters on the pear tree which we planted two years ago; and by the wooden plank which crosses Monty's Leap, the sticky leaves of the trichocarpa exude their exotic scent.

Persian Carpet wallflowers colour the beds around the cottage. Aubretia, white and mauve, fall over moss-covered stones. Dandelions are beginning to prove their invincibility again, piercing the joints of the stones in the path outside the cottage door. Foolish bumble bees buzz against the glass of the porch. A cuckoo, dipping its tail, calls on the rock at Carn Barges. A vixen in the lane in the afternoon warns us that cubs have made her fearless. A wren sings among the willows beside the stream. The first bluebells are in flower down the cliff. A blackbird in the elderberry close to the barn proclaims that she has a nest nearby. Rabbits chase each other in the field opposite. Last year's tadpoles crawl as frogs from hibernating hideouts. The sunset is noticeably further to the west. Woodpigeons hurry to and from the wood, larks sing above the field behind the bridge, small birds perform aerobatics in their excitement, gulls' cries have an enlarged vocabulary. This is May Day. These are the pleasures that have brought happiness to man over the centuries. No computer can halt their repetition, no politician, or shop steward, no passing mood or fashion.

I did not find the swallow nest in the barn for some days. At first I did not want to investigate, fearing my presence might upset this sudden acceptance of Minack as a home. I felt like someone who had sold a house to an enthusiastic buyer, but who was still awaiting the contract. Any little matter might upset the completion of the deal. I had to be careful. If the swallows thought the barn was regularly used, they might also think the place was dangerous. Hence my caution, and Jeannie's, and why we warned Geoffrey not to go into the barn at all during this crucial period when the swallows were settling in. I hoped the donkeys would be equally considerate.

We had acquired Penny one late Spring evening after calling at a pub called the Plume of Feathers at Scorrier, near Redruth. The landlord was also a horse dealer and from time to time sold donkeys; and he had, on the evening we called, this black donkey in a field at the back of the pub waiting for a buyer. She was an Irish donkey imported from Connemara a few months before, and she was not in good condition. But her soulful eyes looked at Jeannie, and Jeannie was conquered, and I said I would buy her. She was also in foal. 'Two donkeys for the price of one,' said the landlord cheerfully as he collected my cheque. We put Penny in the back of the Land Rover and drove back to Minack; and a month later, on the twenty-eighth of May, Fred was born in a field overlooking the sea.

He was now a large donkey. Indeed when people came to see him there was sometimes a note of disappointment in their voices. 'He's bigger than his mother,' they would say doubtfully. And so he was. Penny, while Fred was growing up, was an also ran as far as visitors were concerned. Everybody wanted to take photographs of Fred and Penny just mooched about in the background. But then came the time when Fred lost the luxury of youth, and suddenly someone said; 'I prefer the black donkey.' This became a trend. Penny began receiving the attention which she hitherto had been denied.

Fred, nevertheless, was splendid to look at. He had a fine, intelligent head with a rough coat of chocolate colour in winter, and a shiny smooth chestnut coat in summer. He was, when the swallows arrived, in the changeover period from winter coat to summer coat; and though temporarily he had an untidy appearance, the mark of his cross was as prominent as ever. It was this cross which gave him an advantage over Penny. Penny's cross merged into her black coat. You could hardly see it. Fred's cross was quite clear, winter and summer; the dark line along his back joining the dark lines pointing down his shoulders.

One summer's day a little girl was brought by her mother, a stranger, to see him and Penny. I told the little girl the traditional story of the cross, how Jesus rode into Jerusalem on a donkey and how all donkeys were blessed with a cross ever after. Some while later I had a letter from the mother saying that the child had been seriously ill and had two operations in the Great Ormond Street Hospital for Children in London. It seemed that Fred and his cross had made a great impression on her, and she would murmur about him as she lay in her ward. The mother said that she was now recovering and wanted to give Fred a present . . . carrots came by another post, and inside the parcel there

41

was also a drawing. A primitive picture by the little girl of Fred and his cross.

The donkeys normally ignored the barn in the summer and so it was perverse of them to decide to take notice of it when the swallows arrived. The barn was their winter home. Here they sheltered when the gales raged, here we would spread hay on the cobblestone floor when the grass had lost its bite, here they would stamp and snort as they waited for the weather to clear. But in summer, though they preferred to spend the night in the stable field with its entry to the barn, they never sheltered in the barn itself. A summer storm, and they would stand side by side with bottoms to the hedge, their heads drooping, miserable donkeys looking as if they were in a trance. Yet we had long ago given up the idea that we were doing them a favour when, Mackintoshes over our heads, we dashed out into the rain and led them disconsolately into the barn. Once inside, they soon came out. We were considered a nuisance when we interrupted their wet ruminations.

It was Fred who changed the routine. No sooner had the swallows begun to swoop in and out of the narrow barn door than Fred became curious as to what they were up to. He would disappear inside while Penny, too experienced to be interested in such matters, remained munching among the buttercups. After a minute or two Fred would reappear in the doorway, but instead of coming out into the field to join Penny he would stand stationary, blocking the entrance. It is possible that this was a deliberate act on his part to hinder the swallows, more likely it was a ploy to relieve the tedium of the day. He enjoyed diversions. His floppy ears almost reached the stone lintel of the doorway, and his frame filled the rest of the space. Would he annoy the swallows? Would they twitter angrily with frustration? He was quickly to find out. Each swallow dived at him from a height, and flew into the barn between his floppy ears like supersonic aircraft between two peaks in the Alps.

I was ignorant of the ways of swallows. I had never lived in a house where swallows nested. I knew, of course, that the nest was made of mud, but I had never considered how the nest was lined until one day I was standing on the bridge

42

and saw a swallow playing in the air with a feather. One of
Boris's feathers. Boris's annual moult came at a convenient
time for the birds in the area. He used to squat near his
pond on a bed of London Pride, preening himself, scatter-
ing his under feathers about with abandon; and I now
watched the swallow collect one, then aonther, then another.
It was a gay procedure. Up in the sky above the greenhouse, the swallow would let go of the feather, and the
feather would float in the air while the swallow performed
acrobatics around it before seizing it again, then letting it
go after a yard or two and soaring into the sky, then returning, and at last in serious mood dive with it into the barn. I
was now as curious as Fred. I had to find out the mysterious
spot to which these furnishings were being taken.

I went into the barn one early morning, and promptly a
swallow flew away in fright. I did not notice from which
corner it was startled but I imagined it came from somewhere near the rafters. The nest must surely be attached to
one of the beams. But it was an ancient barn, the plaster
had crumbled away from the slates in the roof, the battens
straddling these slates were in many cases broken, and it
seemed a miracle that the roof had not been blown away
many gales ago. And when I looked up to find the swallow's
nest, I realised suddenly there was no safe place for it to be.
Not directly above me in any case.

There was, however, to the right of where I was standing
a kind of first floor not more than twelve feet square. It was
a haphazard affair reached by ladder, a floor of wooden
planks which rested on the wall at the far end, and an oak
beam which had come from a long ago wreck at my end;
and in between there were three lesser sized cross beams,
and two upright ones which Penny and Fred liked to gnaw
when they were looking for something to do in the winter.
In decades gone by these wooden planks were used for
'shooting' potato seeds, potatoes spread out on the planks
in October and planted in February when they had
sprouted; and while we have been at Minack, they have
been the scene of two minor adventures. Before we came to
live here, we brought Monty, our ginger cat, down from
London for the weekend; and when we were due to return he

was nowhere to be found . . . desperate hours later we discovered him hidden in a cobwebbed corner where the planks rested on the wall. Then Lama hid up there when she was wild, and it was upon one of the planks I placed the first saucer of milk I ever offered her; and which she consumed as soon as I had disappeared. For years, however, we had not made use of the space except to dump things which we believed we might need in the future but never did. I now realised that above all the bric-à-brac must be the nest. The rafters, the batterns, and the plaster were certainly more secure at that end of the barn. And I decided that as I knew the swallows were absent, this was the time to go up and have a look.

The planks were only a foot or two above my head, three rungs up the ladder and I was standing on them. In one corner there were a dozen and more old fashioned wooden flower boxes . . . old fashioned because freight costs had outpriced this once normal way of sending flowers safely to market. Alongside them were rolled up bundles of netting which we once used over the freesias to help the stems to stand upright; and which I remembered buying from an old fisherman who made fishing nets in Porthleven. There were a couple of discarded deck chairs, their once bright orange material punctured with moth eaten holes. I saw an old window frame without its glass; a worn, well-travelled suitcase with faded labels and which would never be used again, a fishing rod, and a tin of weedkiller which should not have been left there and this I would take back with me and throw away. But I saw no swallow's nest.

I came down the ladder and went back to the cottage and saw Jeannie. I told her I could find nothing, and she said I must be blind because the swallows were nesting in the barn without question. I waited until Geoffrey arrived, then he and I went into the barn and had another look; and as we went in a swallow flew out again. Geoffrey, one feels, can deal with most situations that can occur in the countryside. He belongs to one of the oldest families in our parish of St Buryan. His father is a craftsman carpenter and these two, father and son and a little help from outside, built in their spare time two adjacent houses in the valley below Moor-

44

croft between Minack and St Buryan. It was a painstaking effort, and took over four years to complete; and when at last the work was over Geoffrey and his family lived in one half and the other half was occupied by a couple and their child from Wales. Geoffrey's was a splendid house with a great window in the sitting-room looking across the fields and hills to the Ding Dong country on the other side of Penzance. So peaceful was the setting that one could never consider tragedy would be connected with it.

The two of us clambered about the planks and, as I expected, found nothing. I realised that the more frustrated I had become, the noisier I had been; and the anxious, considerate thoughts I had had about the swallows not being disturbed were now being disrupted by my own behaviour . . . I was, in fact, playing the routine role of someone who is unselfish when he is not involved but selfish when he is. We returned to the cobblestone floor and almost immediately Geoffrey said: 'I've found it!' We had been floundering about on the planks looking at the rafters when all the while the nest was just *under* the planks. It was on a ledge of one of the cross beams, and it was not a customary cup-shaped swallow's nest. The packed mud ran along the beam so that the nest was a shallow dip; and the site was open enough and low enough for it to be knocked to pieces by one swipe of an inquisitive donkey's nose. As we stood looking at it one of the swallows flew into the barn, and hovered, twittering, then flew out again in unhappy excitement.

'That,' I said to Geoffrey, 'settles it for the donkeys. They can't come in here this summer. We'll have to keep the bottom half of the door shut.' I heard snorts behind me. Penny and Fred were looking in at us from the doorway, two donkey faces which looked apprehensive. 'Donkeys,' I said, addressing them, 'the barn from now on is out of bounds.' And so it was until the swallows in the autumn flew away to the south.

I was greedy for bird's eggs when I was a boy. I was at a preparatory school called Copthorne not far from East Grinstead; and on my twelfth birthday I was given a small, darkly varnished box so designed inside that there were com-

45

partments for eggs of various sizes. I cherished that box, and I used to carry it along with me on my bird nesting expeditions in the woods around Copthorne, encouraged by a master we called Cobble Wobbles because he was always shaking his head; and who believed that the theft of birds' eggs offered a practical lesson in natural history. I had no qualms that I might be doing wrong because I had been brought up to obey authority without ever challenging it; and Cobble Wobbles was God as far as I was concerned. The more successful I was as a human magpie, jackdaw or carrion crow, the more pleased he was with me; and when the egg collecting season was over I turned to butterfly collecting. Cobble Wobbles would lead the Form on hot summer days, nets in our hands, in exciting chases through the woods after the beautiful, fleeting objects; and there was a sense of triumph when we returned to the school with a record catch of once shimmering loveliness.

I do not remember when my mood changed, when I decided I wanted the life around me to live rather than to die for the sake of providing me with a macabre pleasure. It was a gradual process, not even completed when I first came to Minack; for in the beginning I shot rabbits without thinking of those I failed to kill and which disappeared wounded, into the undergrowth. But if you live in isolated country there comes a time when you have to decide whether your life is to be that of a hunter or a member of an untamed community; and I chose to look upon myself as being one of the latter.

As a child, however, I would have taken one of the swallow eggs; and I would have punctured a hole at each end and cleared it of its yolk. I would have placed it in its chosen hole in the wooden box and would have boasted about what I had done. I would have taken eggs from other nests at Minack, and there would have been one less blackbird to sing, one less thrush, one less green woodpecker to fly dipping its way through the wood. This summer, safe from my childish ghost, the birds had only their own kind to fear. Not even Lama would bother them. Like Monty she had no interest in catching birds.

We used the bridge as a lookout for discovering where

birds were nesting, and we would stand there observing the comings and goings, as if we were observing the activities of a street. There were the thrushes, snug in the evergreen foliage of the camellia just below the shelter. In the shelter itself where we keep the tractor and the garden tools, where the forty-gallon tank of paraffin is stored which we use to keep us warm while we bunch during the daffodil season, a pair of blackbirds had chosen to build their nest on the blade of a scythe; a scythe which had remained unused during the winter but which was urgently required as soon as the blackbirds arrived; we of course did not use it. A wren had chosen a small hole in the wall a couple of feet from the barn door. The chaffinches which stuffed themselves throughout the year on the bird table, had built their tiny nest in the gorse bush beside the lane opposite the door of the old stable which I use as an office. A pair of robins had created a cup of dried grass between two stones in the wall close to the white gate through which we take the donkeys into the field above the cottage. The magpies, as usual, were in the blackthorn copse towards Carn Barges, and, as usual, I resented their presence though admiring their splendid plumage. An ornithologist told me once that one need never be ashamed of shooting a magpie or a carrion crow; and one was justified in taking their eggs, the exception to prove the rule, because of the appetite they had for small birds. Yet each year would go by and I would do nothing, an example of confused thinking; for on the one hand I wanted to safeguard the lives of birds, yet on the other hand I was avoiding taking action against those who killed them. But where would the list end? Hawks, jackdaws, buzzards would also have to be on the list if I were to take the task seriously; and I would become like a lady I know who believes that a vital duty of her life is to destroy wasp nests . . . friends and acquaintances from miles around notify her as soon as a wasp nest is discovered, and the lady jumps into her car, however inconvenient the hour, and hastens with her poison to the offending nest. It was easier for me, I decided, to let nature look after itself; at any rate until I had visual evidence to enrage me.

Around the meadow where stands the small greenhouse

is a circle of elm trees, and each year a pair of green wood-peckers nests in one of them, a pair of tawny owls in another. The owls, of course, are very secretive; and I never know for certain they are there, though passing the tree every day, until the time has come for the young to fly . . . and then one early morning I become aware I am being watched, the watcher being one of the parents in the willows opposite the tree where the young, one or two, have been brought up in a hollow. Each year it is the same hollow. Once a baby owl fell out in some mysterious way and we found it alive, a white feathered object the size of a child's fist, at the base of the tree with a dead mouse beside it. The parents, presumably, unable to get it back to the nest, were making a futile effort to look after it where it lay. We picked it up, climbed up the tree, and placed it in the hollow alongside another; and a few weeks later we saw deep in the wood two young owls sitting on a branch, side by side like Tweedle Dum and Tweedle Dee. But this summer there was only one young owl. I first saw him perched on the top of Boris's hut when I was on the way to open the door in the morning, still so young that curiosity overcame the sense of possible danger; and because I did not want to disillusion his trust I decided to leave Boris inside for a moment, and went on past the hut further into the wood. Out of the corner of my eye I saw him continue to stare at me, turning his head in human fashion to follow me as I passed. Yet in a week or two I realised, he would be frightened by the sight of me, and he would be gliding away silently between the branches of the trees, miraculously silent; and I contemplated, as I passed him, that the trust he now had in me was a reflection of all the innocents, the original trust. Talent and brains are distributed unevenly, and so is good fortune. Trust is the only quality the new-born momentarily share.

The circle of elms are pockmarked with holes that have been tapped out of the trees by past generations of green woodpeckers, and one of the holes is chosen each year for redecoration. The chosen hole this year was fifteen feet from the ground between the small greenhouse and Boris's hut, and the rim of its entrance was freshly pecked as if it were a newly painted front door. I feel sure the woodpeckers would like to keep their nesting habits as secretive as the owls but their characteristics make it impossible. They are, for instance, so exotic to look at. The crimson crown and green plumage are striking enough to attract attention under any circumstances, the more so when the trees are bare of leaves; and as the leaves are always late in our part of Cornwall, there is no cover for them to hide in when the nesting period begins. They are noisy too. They draw attention to themselves time and again by calling out their rapidly repeated note whenever they believe danger is about; and the note sounds on these occasions like a nervous laugh. So everyone knows when the woodpeckers arrive to nest at Minack, including the two carrion crows who have their headquarters at the other end of the wood.

There was another nest this year in this circle of elms. Three elms from that of the woodpeckers, high up on a fork of the tree, was a mistlethrush's nest. I had watched two courting while we were bunching the late daffodils, and I hoped they would stay in the neighbourhood because the mistlethrush, or storm cock as it is called, has a special significance for us. It is a bird of the gales. I have seen it on days when I have had to bend double to fight my way into the wind, when our gulls have been too scared to parade on the roof . . . I have seen it defying the weather, perched on the elder down by the stream, singing its song into the storm. A bird which, in such circumstances, brings reassurance. So I was glad that it had chosen to nest with us; and we felt it a compliment in an undefinable way.

Mistlethrush, woodpecker, swallow . . . these were the nests which interested us most. Only the swallows were to be safe.

SIX

The jackdaws hunt in packs during May and June, and
sometimes they come swarming over Minack cackling with
greedy cries. Their home is less than half a mile away in a
cliff which falls sheer to the sea, a mass of crevices providing hideouts over the centuries. The cottage where Jane lived
is close by; and the small meadow where she used to go on
moonlit nights to dig the soil with the Cornish longhandled
shovel and plant her bulbs which still flower there in the
spring, lies to the side of the cliff half way down, a pocket
of unexpected land only reached by those who know the
secret route. Commandos were once trained to climb this

50

cliff, approaching it by boat from Newlyn, and clambering ashore on the rocks, then up to the top with uncanny speed. In early summer they faced the angry jackdaws as they climbed between the nests, and I met a commando who, after he had been dived at and pecked at, said vehemently: 'I'd rather be shot at by humans.'

We, therefore, fear the jackdaws when they come to Minack because they sweep into the trees and bushes, hopping nimbly but inquisitively from branch to branch, cackling ceaselessly, inevitably threatening all the fledgling and egg-filled nests in the neighbourhood. Yet we know it is partly our fault that they come. All through the year we have a jackdaw or two on watch near the cottage, ready to seize any scraps we throw to the gulls on the roof, that the gulls do not like or are too slow to take. We accept the presence of these jackdaws, even regret that they remain so wary of us, because we are bemused by their beady eyes as they wait alertly the chance to dart at a delicacy. But at nesting time these jackdaws proceed to act as scouts on behalf of their colleagues, sending them a message as soon as we have put food on the roof or grain on the ground for the small birds. Thus, just as a gull is deliberating whether or not to slide on its bottom from the apex of the roof to the bacon rind lodged near the gutter, a bevy of jackdaws suddenly appears overhead.

The first gull on the roof was called Hubert; and he had been visiting us for a long time when one day he arrived with a leg dangling, and blood on his feathers. He had been shot by a boy with an airgun on the rocks where he roosted; and there was nothing we could do to save him. Then there was Gregory, a gull with one leg, the other no doubt lost in a gin trap which is now illegal; and he used to wait on the other side of the shallow valley, a white spot in the field, until dusk was falling and he felt safe to fly to the roof without the likelihood of being attacked by another gull . . . we never saw him again after a gale which raged for two days. And there was Knocker. Knocker was a very intelligent gull who rapped his beak on the roof with such purpose whenever he required attention that strangers in the cottage were apt to say: 'There's someone knocking at the

51

door.' Knocker too has now disappeared.

Knocker used to come to the roof in the company of a gull we named Squeaker because she was always making a hiccuping, squeaking noise like a young gull just out of the nest. Squeaker still comes to the roof, and she still squeaks. She flies up from Lamorna Cove direction; and she has a new companion, Peter, who is so nervous when he is on the roof that any wideawake jackdaw pounces first on the food we have given him. Philip is our favourite gull because he has a detached attitude towards life, a gull who likes to contemplate a great deal on his own, and when we see him musing away up on the chimney we have the impression that he is often sagely thinking about us below him as we go about our business. He is fussy about his food and will have nothing to do with shop bread. He is very fond of bacon and in the summer when we are having breakfast outside on the bridge and the breakfast consists of bacon and eggs, Philip is certain to be within a few feet of us, beak watering, waiting for the inevitable choice portion to be given to him.

Both Knocker and Philip were victims of the *Torrey Canyon* oil, and Philip was the worse sufferer of the two. Knocker was filmed with oil, Philip when I first saw him had his underparts saturated. The sight of them both naturally enraged me but the sight of Philip also surprised me. He was the first *Torrey Canyon* victim I had seen but I knew at the time that the main oil slick still had not reached my part of the Cornish coast. Hence Philip must have collected his oil some distance off Land's End and what was he doing so far away? We treated him in the only way we could. We bought him five pounds in weight of bacon during the course of the following week. He stuffed himself on it; and it gave him strength to perform his own cleaning and the fat, it seemed, countered the effects of any oil he might swallow in doing so. Within three weeks he looked his old self, and so also did Knocker and they were both wise enough to stop wandering afar while the *Torrey Canyon* affair lasted. There was never any oil on the rocks along our stretch of Mount's Bay, and so they were safe if they stayed in the neighbourhood. Our own particular hell was

52

watching the guillemots. We could see them floundering off-shore, struggling needlessly to reach the supposed safety of our rocks . . . needlessly because they had become so soaked with oil long before coming within sight of our own rocks that there was no chance of them living.

Nor was there any chance of the young mistlethrushes living. The nest was as obvious as a television mast attached to a lonely house. There were no leaves on the elm to camouflage the nest when the eggs were laid or when they were hatched. The nest sat on the fork of a tree for all in the sky to see; and although the leaves were fat on the branches a week before the birds were ready to fly, they had blossomed too late. The jackdaws, and the two carrion crows at the other end of the wood, had already marked down the nest; and its occupants were doomed.

It was ironic, therefore, that we should help the jackdaws with their own nests. Or Penny did. The jackdaws apparently considered her black hair as an enviable adornment to their nests on the cliff and when they came to Minack in search for food, they also showed a desire to acquire part of Penny for their furnishings. I would look out of the bathroom which faces the big field, and observe two jackdaws with their grey heads resembling quaint grey hats, perched on the rump of Penny pecking at her coat until their beaks were so full that they appeared to be wearing moustaches. Penny never objected, behaving all the while as if she were flattered that her black coat was in such demand. We, on the other hand, faced with the bare patch at the end of the nest-making season, had to make excuses on her behalf and, for that matter on our own behalf. The bare patch looked as if she had mange, and we would notice visitors staring at it with disapproval. 'It's the jackdaws,' we would explain apologetically, 'she allows them to take the hairs, you see. She doesn't mind at all.'

Fred minded. The jackdaws showed no interest whatsoever in his upholstery. His winter coat which he was only too anxious to be rid of, had a fine texture which one would have imagined was ideally suited for any nest. But it was the wrong colour, and so the jackdaws passed him by. This annoyed him. Fred indeed, always minds when Penny re-

53

ceives more attention than he does; though it is not jealousy that causes him to feel so. It is just that he wants to join in the fun. Penny hurt her foot one day and the vet came out to inspect it; and as he was inspecting it along came Fred. He was tossing his head about in a way which denotes that he has found something to laugh at. Snorts reflect his laughter, and up he came to the vet snorting his head off. 'Go away Fred,' said the vet, and I, who was holding Penny, gave Fred a push. Thereupon Fred collapsed on the grass within a few feet of us, rolled on his back displaying his large tummy, and keeping his eye on us as if he was saying: 'Look at me, aren't I worth your attention?' He behaves like a clown when he is wanting notice. Life in his opinion is very funny.

Penny, meanwhile, is a lady who enjoys poor health when she has a chance to enjoy it. Her foot, so the vet explained to us, had a slight sprain and no more. Yet it was far too much trouble to walk even a few steps towards us when we brought her carrots and chocolate biscuits. Indeed her interpretation of the role of an invalid was so exaggerated that she would lie comfortably in the furthest corner of the field expecting us to walk to her, kneel beside her, and push our offerings into her mouth. This desultory behaviour would naturally have alarmed us had we not had the reassurance of the vet that there was nothing to worry about; and also the added evidence of our own eyes when we saw her, a few minutes after we had disappeared from her sight, gadding about the field like a two-year-old. Ill-health for Penny was an entertainment.

The jackdaws and the carrion crows ravaged the mistle-thrush nest in the third week of May, a week before Fred's birthday. I have a feeling that one of the carrion crows started the attack, and that the jackdaws joined in. I had woken up to the sound of the cows being called in for milking by my friend Jack, one of the farmers at the top of the lane, and I saw through the bedroom window that it was a lovely early morning, and I was cross with myself for not waking sooner. I lay there for a moment looking out through the window, and listened to a thrush singing ebulliently, and then with irritation to the harsh caw-caw-caw of the carrion crow. I would have continued lazily to lie there had it not been for Lama who came in from the sitting-room where she had been sleeping and proceeded to tell me to get up. I never know whether Lama is waking me up because she wants to go outside, or whether it is a selfish desire to have her breakfast, or whether she is performing a favour by drawing to our reluctant attention that a beautiful early morning awaits us. The hour depends on the daylight, and so in mid-summer I can expect to hear her beside me at five in the morning. She comes to the side of the bed and makes a tiny strangled cry as if she is being garotted; or she is content with a squeak that sounds like: 'Ee-Ee'. Both have a penetrating effect.

I seldom, however, display any immediate reaction. I hear the noise in my half sleep, and try to make up my mind as to the significance of the sound. If I decide it is prompted by greed, I bring out my hand from under the bedclothes, make contact with her, and give her a push. I promptly regret my action though hoping that as a result she will now be silent. She isn't. The strangled cry is repeated. So also the 'ee-ee'. And they are repeated again and again and again until I clamber out of bed.

We have the wire-framed contraption across our open window at night that we had made for Monty. He used to be free to go out through the window at night until we found a fox waiting for him directly under the window sill; and then his freedom was curtailed, as Lama's freedom is curtailed. Thus I often suspect that Lama, when she wakes us up, is taking revenge for the discipline we impose upon her. She remembers the mouse she nearly caught the previous evening and she wants to return to the hole where she knows it is hiding. Or she just wants to go a-wandering because it is a lovely morning; and she is comforted by the thought that *she* at any rate will be able to catch up on her sleep during the day. Whatever her wishes may be it is our job to obey them. However reluctantly.

On this occasion, however, she was surprised by my pleasant welcome. I clambered out of bed murmuring flattering noises at her, then, much to her delight, I went to the fridge and brought out the saucer of John Dorey fish, part of which she had relished the previous evening. A few minutes later I was outside my dressing gown, shuffling down the path of grey chippings in my bedroom slippers, looking across the valley for the cubs I expected to see; and filling my lungs with the air coming off the sea, and grass growing scents, and those of wallflowers, and that of the verbena by the white seat.

It was a Saturday, and on Saturdays during the summer the *Scillonian* makes a double trip to the Scilly Isles; the first leaves Penzance at six in the morning and returns about mid-day, then sets out again at half past one. But it is the morning trip which always intrigues me. How is she so full? Who are these people who crowd her decks at such an early hour of the morning? I watched her sail by Minack, loving the white smartness of her hull, and the way she provides in a turbulent world evidence that a duty can be honoured; for whatever the storms and the strain of the crew, she will keep to her schedule so that the islanders can be sure their produce arrives on the mainland. I watched her disappearing out of sight behind the may tree, soon to bloom, that edges the path on the way down to the cemetery field and the cliff, when I was startled by the commotion among the elms on my left.

It was a terrible noise, similar in its tone of hysteria to that of a pack of hounds after a cornered fox, only it wasn't the noise of howls that filled the air but that of a ghastly cackling; and it was high up. Of course I didn't have to think twice to know what was happening, and I ran towards the tree clapping my hands and shouting. I could do no more. I couldn't climb the tree and if I had fetched a ladder it wouldn't have been any use. The nest was destroyed in a matter of seconds. There would be no young storm cocks to shout their songs into the gales next winter.

The incident was a warning as to what might happen to the woodpeckers. Nothing could hurt them at the moment because they were safe deep in the hole, but as the days went by they grew mature enough to become inquisitive, and they began poking their heads out of the hole. One in particular we noticed; and no doubt he had been the first of the brood to be hatched. His was the head which was frequently framed in the hole, and we could see others of the brood jostling for position behind him. His excitement was always greatest when one of the parents was in the neighbourhood about to bring to the nest the result of a foraging expedition, and then he would make a burbling note which was a miniature version of a woodpecker's laugh. He was still quite safe. A carrion crow or a jackdaw could not enter the hole. No doubt its whereabouts had been marked, no doubt that the signs that the woodpeckers were growing up had been observed. But no attacks on them could be made until they left the hole on their first wavering flight.

Fred, meanwhile, had received fifty-two cards on his birthday, and most of them came from the children of St Buryan. The village of St Buryan is three miles away from us, and it is a sturdy village which has an atmosphere that suggests it has an inbred awareness of its past. Historically it dates back to the sixth century when an Irish girl saint called Berian travelled this way and founded a shrine in the then encampment; and later in the tenth century King Athelstan, after defeating the Danes at Boleigh Hill, worshipped at the shrine before setting out with his army from the beaches of Sennen to drive the Danes from the Scilly Isles. He made a vow, when he was at the shrine that he would endow and build a church at St Buryan if the expedition was successful. He kept his vow, and the original church lasted until the fifteenth century; then the present one was built, a beautiful building with a fine tower which in the days of sail was a landmark for ships far out to sea. Yet it is not just the historical aspect which gives St Buryan its strength. This is a village which has belonged so much to the soil, the storms, the droughts, the daily struggle of living with nature over the centuries that the villagers whose families have lived here for generations are instinctively loyal to the basic values. They hold firm opinions, are kind and generous, but are never strident. Outsiders are now coming to live in the village, and whereas five years ago there were only solid granite cottages to live in, one now sees on the outskirts an increasing number of bungalows with outside walls faced with *ersatz* stone. Old men, sitting on the bench in front of the church, see someone go by and do not know their name; old men on the same bench a few years ago knew the intimate personal story of everyone they saw.

We buy our weekly groceries at St Buryan from the shop which is simply called the Shop. ('I'm going up shop' say the locals). It is run by a couple called Lily and Ted Chapple who offer that personal service to their customers that a computer might tell them was uneconomic. They know the special whims and fancies of all who come to them, young and old; and at Christmas time they follow a custom that the computer would certainly condemn. Each regular customer receives a present, and a handsome one at that. The Shop is indeed in tune with the character of St Buryan, though it now has to compete with a flush of supermarkets that national chains have introduced into Penzance after buying up old fashioned concerns. Tempting advertisements, promising twopence off this and fourpence off that, try to lure the ladies of St Buryan to transfer their allegiance from the Shop to Penzance. There is, however, the bus fare to be paid; and the personal attention to be lost.

Across the road from the Shop are the pub and the Post Office. We used to go regularly to the pub in the days of the landlord called Jim Grenfell; and ten years ago before the mains were brought to the village, I used to stand at the bar window watching the villagers queueing up with their pails to collect water from the village well opposite. The pub has now been redesigned, and the present landlord is known as one of the most welcoming in West Cornwall, but we seldom go there ourselves. There is no fun now in going to the village pub if you live outside the village. Instead of having a roistering time, there you are standing by the bar clinically deciding whether the law will allow you another half pint. Maybe it is a worthy law but it is a law that has resulted in the loss of a legion of friendships. And the teetotallers drive as fast as ever.

The Post Office is presided over by Leslie Payne, a kind man whose occasional vagueness endears him to the many who appreciate his gentle character. His courtesy is famous and if you are engaged in some post office business, you may find yourself being offered a sweet from a large tin. He takes infinite trouble with any inquiry and, if you are accustomed to some city post offices, you will regret that Leslie Payne is not your local postmaster. He also sells fruit and vegetables, sweets and a few groceries and also newspapers. We have our Sunday newspapers from him, but he does not have a high opinion of newspapers. 'Another load of rubbish,' he will say as he hands the bundle over to us. Or during the week he may hand us, instead of the paper of the day, an out-of-date issue saying we will not notice the difference. He also sells ice-cream and on Fred's birthday this summer he organised Fred's customary gift to every child in the school.

It was a beautiful morning, and we were up soon after the sun rose across the bay above the Lizard peninsula, and from our bedroom window we could see a clump of mackerel boats off-shore, their owners trying to make a catch for the morning market at Newlyn. The donkeys were in the field above the cottage, the field now yellow with buttercups, and we went out in dressing gowns to call them. 'Fred!' I shouted, 'Fred!' When he was born our vet nicknamed him His Nibs and he still calls him this. 'How is His Nibs?' he will ask when we see him in Penzance. His Nibs, on this occasion, came across the field at the gallop leaving Penny far behind him. Penny is always more lethargic, realising I suppose that there is all the time in the world for anything she decides to do. 'Happy birthday!' we both called, and I found myself thinking that no time had gone by since last year, and the year before, and the year before that. The same pattern. The same instant of pleasure. And for Fred the same eating delights awaiting him.

In due course, before they had to hurry off to school, Susan and Janet from the farm at the top of the lane arrived at the cottage. Both have known Fred since he was born, and every summer they remember, and bring him a special birthday card, and a bunch of carrots; and this summer they brought with them the school birthday cards as well.

They were really drawings, not cards, and one was a four foot long poster with the message: HAPPY BIRTHDAY FREDDY FROM ALL IN CLASS 3. Each member of this junior class had helped to draw against the backcloth of a green field a Breughel-style version of children at a donkey's party; merry colours, movement, humour and tremendous gaiety. There were drawings with splashes of colours that an adult would have been frightened to use unless he did so with self-conscious intention; and the designs were equally free from inhibitions. A drawing with an ice-cream in one corner, carrots galore, a chocolate cake with candles on it, all in reds, greens, blues, browns, yellows and the message: ONLY THE BEST DONKEY IN THE WORLD COULD EXPECT THIS CARD. Another of a donkey in a field at night with dark clouds overhead except for a patch in the sky where the full moon is bright. Another of a donkey in a stable made of carrots. Another of a donkey in a field with carrots floating about in the sky. Another decorated with butterflies, cakes and hearts. Another of a donkey wearing bright yellow harness and carrying a purple pannier. Endless messages of HUGS AND KISSES, LOTS OF LOVE, I HOPE YOU HAVE A HAPPY BIRTHDAY WITH LOTS OF CARROTS. And some of the drawings showed Fred smoking a pipe. It is his parlour trick. And a few of the children had once seen him performing it. We treated these greetings with the solemnity they deserved, and after we had had our breakfast, we read them out to the donkeys and pushed the drawings against their white noses. This charade which we have performed each year has a special purpose, for it is a gesture to the children for the efforts they have made; and the donkeys, of course, are quite ready to tolerate our foolish behaviour. After a few drawings have been pushed against their noses, we give them an interval in which they sample their presents.

The lush period of summer had now begun. Young green bracken was thrusting through the thickening grass, through the mass of leaves of the fading bluebells, draping the sides of lanes and blanketing the moorland, hiding paths which were once easy to find. Coarse docks and thistles sprouted in the daffodil meadows among the dying foliage of the daffodils. Ought we not to be efficient daffodil growers and keep the meadows sprayed with herbicides instead of relying on the motor mower in due course to cut them down? But we prefer to let the wild flowers be free, the good ones and the bad ones, and in June this summer the insects were humming in the meadows, butterflies stretched out their wings on useless weeds, chattering whitethroats clung to the thistles pecking at the first seeds. Up the lane from the cottage the stream had already become a trickle across Monty's Leap, the may tree beyond the gate on the right was a dome of white scented petals; nettles and foxgloves, Queen Anne's lace, clouds of pink campion and inevitable cow parsley filled the verges and the ditches. And the leaves were now thick on the branches of the elm where the nest of the mistlethrushes used to be, and on the branches around the woodpeckers' hole out of which the eldest one, at any moment, would be ready to fly.

The window of the bathroom looks out on to the donkey field with the wood running along the right, the first part of which contains the elms. There is also, close by, a pole which carries our electric cable to another pole in the wood in one direction and to a spike plunged into the ancient end wall of the cottage in the other direction; and the end wall is where our spare room and bathroom connects to the main cottage. I have never been happy about this arrangement. We both hate the sight of the cable threading its way through the wood and across the field; and we both fear, though we are assured our fears are groundless, that the gales which swing the cable, will produce a swing one day so vicious that the spike will bring the end wall down in a pile of debris. Meanwhile the birds like the cable, especially the swallows as we were to learn, because it is a convenient place to perch; and the carrion crows like the poles because they can sit there high above the trees observing, like big brother, every activity.

I was shaving in the bathroom, looking at my face in an inadequately small mirror, when there was the same hysterical cackling sound that I had heard a few weeks before. It was obvious what was happening, and I glanced quickly out of the window before dashing to the backdoor. Sure enough, I saw through the window that two carrion crows and the jackdaws were fighting over something up there on the electricity pole; and by the time I got through the door and had run into the field, clapping my hands and shouting, the fight had become a din; and it only became silent after they saw me, after they had dropped with a thud the object

61

they had been fighting over, after the jackdaws had hurried away, after the carrion crows, cawing, had left for the far part of the wood.

The object was our young woodpecker. They had watched and waited and caught him on his first flight.

DEREK TANGYE
ST. BURYAN, PENZANCE

Tomatoes Grown for Flavour

SEVEN

In summer we depend on tomatoes to earn us money. The prices are good in May and June, they dip in July, they dip steeply in August. In May and June we gaze at the green fruit on the trusses, willing them to turn pink quickly.

We have five greenhouses (in professional language we have one greenhouse and four mobile greenhouses), and also the small one surrounded by elms which we use now only as a packing shed. At first we used this small one, thirty feet long and twelve feet wide, both as a packing shed and for tomato growing; daffodil bunching and packing in the spring, cold house tomatoes in the summer. The tomatoes proved to be a modest success. There was a holiday demand locally, and so there was no problem about disposing

63

of the crop; and most important from a cost point of view there was no carriage to pay as there was with flowers and potatoes.

This modest success gave us ideas about changing our pattern of growing. We had become disenchanted with potatoes as a summer crop. Year after year at some crucial time of the potato growing season there would either be a violent gale or an exceptional frost; and our crop would be laid waste. Apparently we were living at the time in a ten-year cycle of such weather. The year we stopped growing potatoes, the harvest was bountiful. It has been bountiful ever since.

It is easy to forget the anguish that surrounds past endeavours. That last summer of potato growing we had hoped to harvest twenty-eight tons of potatoes, and we harvested twelve tons instead. We were as near defeat as we have ever been at Minack. There have been many times when we did not possess the cash to pay for our groceries, or for petrol, or for a drink at the pub. The bills and our hopes would mount up as we waited for a potato or flower harvest to mature; and the harvest would seldom equal our bills and our hopes, and so little would be left to carry us forward. We were maddening to our families. They grew exasperated with our optimism. For weeks before a daffodil or a potato season we would regale them with our high expectations; and then they would notice a silence while the season was in progress; and then, monotonously, they would receive our report after the season was over, a report that the weather had been the worst that old men in the district could remember. The harvest, whichever it was, had failed.

Yet Jeannie never wavered in her confidence that one day all would be well. It was I who became jumpy. I remember one desperate occasion when I seized my gun, not with the dramatic intention of shooting myself, but in an unreasoned, hysterical gesture of protest against the fates. Unfortunately in my rage I raised the butt of the gun so savagely that it hit my mouth; and to this day I have a damaged tooth which my dentist threatens to remove each time I visit him.

a mocking version of the kind of life we led. It was hateful. It was particularly hateful for Jeannie because there were various jokes in the play of a domestic nature; and the set of the play (a friend recognised the interior of the cottage from the photographs of the set outside the theatre) accentuated the primitive way with which she had to cope with guests. A feature was that we had no sink; and this was made a great joke in the play. In one Act the heroine, after doing the washing up in a basin, carried the basin to the side of the stage and through the front door, then emptied it into the garden (just as we used to do). As the lady performed the task, the audience roared with laughter. We sat by ourselves in the cottage hearing that laughter.

A writ for libel was served on our behalf in due course, and the play was withdrawn after five weeks. The legal wrangle over the libel suit, however, meandered on. The management denied responsibility, arguing they had accepted the play in good faith; and the fact the authors lived in New York further complicated matters. The costs began to mount. We hadn't a penny for an evening out, let alone for an armoury of lawyers; and we became more and more enraged that as a result of the hospitality we had dispensed on that week-end visit, we had now been placed in such an invidious position. Heaven knows what would have happened had not that knight of losing causes, A. P. Herbert, come to our aid. We had known him for many years, and had shared many an incongruous adventure; and he had stayed with us at Minack and been quite unruffled by the then inconveniences. When he heard of our predicament, he marched into the offices of the theatrical management concerned, declared that he was on our side; and he would be glad for the world to know it.

The case was settled within a week; and the judge who announced the settlement, listened to the apologies read out on behalf of the offenders, and proclaimed that Jeannie and I were to receive 'substantial damages.' They were not as substantial as this sounds, nor as substantial as they might have been if we had had the tenacity to take the case to court. But it was enough. The first thing we did was to arrange for the water from the well to be piped to the cottage, then buy an Esse stove . . . and have a sink.

We were fortunate enough to have a kindly bank manager when we decided to have greenhouses. Perhaps his patience had been exhausted by the stories of our woes, and therefore he was in the mood to be receptive to this new idea; for we dazzled him with facts and figures of our financial prospects were we able to possess greenhouses. At any rate he loaned us the deposits. The instalments we were ready to worry about later.

We had pointed out to him that wind, and the salt it carried, was the most persistent danger to our crops; and so if, in the equable Cornish climate, our crops were protected by glass we would have guaranteed, factory produced results. Thus we would be able to grow flowers or lettuces in the winter, and tomatoes in the summer; and we would be able to leave our hazardous potato career behind us. We began with a splendid greenhouse with cement foundations, a hundred feet long and twenty-two feet wide; then later two mobiles each seventy feet long and eighteen feet wide; then another two mobiles seventy feet long and twenty feet wide.

The sight of them was impressive. The fixed greenhouses in front of the cottage, the mobiles in the field beyond. This field had been rocky and uneven, and we had to bulldoze the rocks away and level the site for the mobiles. Unfortunately the field was not long enough for us to gain the full benefit of the mobiles. Ideally a mobile should have three or four sites. Each of our seventy foot mobiles had only two. If we had four, for instance, we might have grown early, middle and late varieties of daffodils, winching the mobile along the rails on its very small wheels to cover each site as one variety succeeded another; and still have been able to grow tomatoes on the fourth site. Hence for the same capital expenditure we would have had four crops.

As we only had the two sites, however, we were forced to decide upon the most profitable crop to dovetail with the tomatoes; and we tried at various times forget-me-nots, chrysanthemums, lettuces, Beauty of Nice stocks, wall-flowers, iris, polyanthus and freesias. Freesias were the most satisfactory until over-production everywhere brought

68

down the price and made them uneconomical; and there
was in any case a snag about freesias. Their picking time
began in January (we had heat by now in the greenhouses)
and the picking reached its peak during March. Hence the
tomato planting had to be delayed because the mobiles were
covering the freesias; and the consequence of this was that
we missed the high tomato prices of June. There came a
time, therefore, when we decided to give up such winter
flower growing. We would devote all our efforts to the
tomatoes.

Today the mobiles have become static greenhouses. We
no longer winch them from one site to another; and though
outsiders sometimes gaze at the bare soil in the winter and
declare that we are not showing economic good sense, that
we are failing to earn the interest on our capital, it seems
we are conducting the right policy. It is wiser to be idle;
and the idleness is also a benefit to the tomatoes. For during
the winter the soil is sterilised by a chemical powder rotovated into the earth, and this has to be left undisturbed for
several weeks with the green-houses kept closed so that the
fumes do not escape. The advantage gained by this can
mean an extra two pounds a plant; and this in terms of
money, can equal the returns of a winter crop. This, and the
fact that the tomatoes are planted in good time, justifies the
barren sight of our greenhouses in winter.

There are other advantages too. We plant the tomatoes
at the beginning of March when the daffodil rush is on, and
so when the sterilisation has been done we can make pre-
parations. Vast quantities of peat are rotovated into the
soil, and also fertilisers that are based on the soil analysis
carried out by the Ministry of Agriculture in the autumn.
Then, in the waiting time of early January, the strings are
tied to the overhead wires that stretch from end to end of
each greenhouse above where the rows of tomato plants
will be. Each plant has this five-ply string to support it,
and the earth end of the string is tied to a short galvanised
stake which is plunged into the ground alongside the plant.
The plants come from a specialist grower near Truro who
delivers them in relays in his van. Everything is ready when
they arrive. We may be in a period when there is a deluge

of daffodils. It doesn't matter. No switchover from a winter flower crop. The tomato plants will be cossetted from their beginning.

This summer we grew two and a half thousand plants, and we chose a type called Moneycross and another called Maascross because both these types tasted like true tomatoes. This age of uniformity has cast its spell on tomatoes like everything else; and this summer it was officially decreed that when tomatoes reached the shops each pack must contain tomatoes of the same size. Government appointed inspectors now cruise around the wholesale markets checking that growers have obeyed the orders to pack their produce according to the official grades; and they will downgrade any pack which does not come up to their standards. These standards are outlined in a booklet which growers are expected to keep handy as they rush to send their harvest to market. The top grade, we are told for instance, must fall 'within one of the following size ranges as measured by the maximum tranverse diameter of the fruits'.

A. 77mm (3 in.) and above but less than 87mm (3 7/16 in.) and so on down to F.

F. 35 mm (1 3/8 in.) and above but less than 40 mm (1 9/16 in.).

The instructions continue: 'The size range packed must, be marked on the container, either in millimetres or inches showing the minimum and maximum for the range (the lower figure to be stated first) or by the appropriate code.'

There are a further three grades each diminishing the standard required. No mention is made of flavour. If the shape fits the grade, the tomato can taste of soap or of nothing at all; and so the housewife, oblivious of the pressures directed upon her buying habits, comes to believe that a neat, uniform plate of tomatoes on the table is an emblem of wise buying. It happens, however, that the tomato varieties most used for uniformity have no flavour; top grade they may be, and of exquisite shape, but they are tasteless.

Jeannie and I soon lost patience with the grading instructions; and we devised a means to circumvent them. We decided to have two grades of our own choice; and on the little piece of paper, stuck to the container, that officialdom demanded should show the grade code number, I put the figure '2' or the word 'small'. The latter described all the very small tomatoes we sent away, while the figure '2' described the rest. Now by marking our tomatoes as second grade we had an immediate advantage. We were saved from any pedantic complaints about the size and shape of our tomatoes which an inspector might make; the tomatoes had to be of very poor standard indeed to be considered third grade. On the other hand we were not doing our tomatoes justice. Hence we had invented a slogan. In bold red letters printed on a card with my name on it, which was stapled to the container alongside the little piece of grading paper, was the slogan:

TOMATOES GROWN FOR FLAVOUR.

It worked wonders. Supermarket minded shops continued to stock the uniform tomatoes; but the others, the small shopkeepers, the hotels and restaurants, made special requests for ours. They were in great demand, and the wholesaler was delighted. And the inspector said nothing. The price we received always topped his Grade 1.

We also took care to grade the tomatoes according to ripeness. I let Geoffrey do the picking because he was faster doing it than I had ever been. I even persuaded myself that my presence and my fumbling slowed his work, and that he felt happier on his own. I preferred to be with Jeannie and deal with the tomatoes when Geoffrey brought them to us in baskets. It was certainly a cleaner job. Tomato foliage acts like a dye; and so when you make your way between the rows, either when pinching out unwanted shoots or when picking the fruit, everything about you becomes green . . . green clothes, green hands, green face. At the end of a morning's picking, Geoffrey's eyebrows were green. He never complained. He would empty the baskets, having first weighed each one so as to keep a record of the output from each greenhouse, then he would proceed to grade them, tak-

71

ing special notice of their colour. I am sure this helped us to collect the best price. A buyer always knew he would never have ripe tomatoes mixed with near ripe ones.

By the middle of June, this summer, it seemed we would have a good season. We were receiving 2s. 6d. a pound, or 30s. a chip (we call a container a chip); and we were despatching to the wholesaler in Penzance one hundred and fifty chips a week. Had such an output continued it would have been splendid but it didn't happen that way. The peak period lasts about three weeks, then tails off, and so do the prices; and against the tomato income we have to balance the cost of the oil for the heaters, two thousand gallons or more; and the four hundred gallons of liquid fertiliser which is fed to the plants throughout the summer by the automatic irrigation; and the cost of the plants at £42 a thousand; and the price of chips at 9d. each; and the cost of peat, basic fertilisers and the sterilisation powder; and of course the price of Geoffrey's labour and our own. Tomatoes, therefore, are our bread and butter, and not a way to a fortune.

This summer the tomatoes had, in fact, been late in coming into market ripeness. We had invested in a new heating system which we thought would be foolproof in its efficiency. Each house had a heater of its own, burning on oil, and the heat was circulated by a powerful fan through perforated polythene ducting that was fixed along the inside of each house. The heaters were automatic. Each house had a thermostat which controlled the temperature required; and the theory was that once the heaters were installed the tomato plants would grow in an ideal artificial environment.

Unfortunately the heaters, though expertly installed, refused to fulfil their function. For one mysterious reason or another, the heaters took turns to break down during the crucial period of the sharp March and April nights. Machines have often broken down at Minack. Second-hand machines or machines delivered straight from the factory, have brought despair to mechanics and to ourselves. The faults are always unusual, always unique. Hence when the heating engineer expressed amazement that the heaters should behave so temperamentally, I myself displayed no

72

surprise. I had long ago become familiar with the sentence which followed:

'Never in all my experience,' said the man vehemently, 'have I known this happen before. Never . . . and I've been in this game for thirty years.'

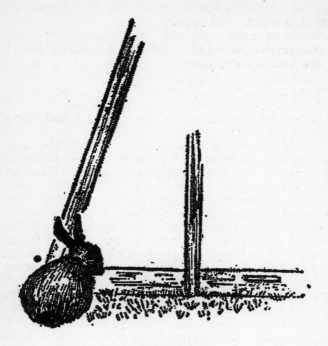

EIGHT

I soon became exasperated by the time involved in dealing with the consequences of the breakdowns . . . letters, telephone calls, telegrams, hours just staring at the offending heaters, more hours having sterile discussions with Geoffrey about them, waiting for engineers to call, forcing myself to make jocular remarks as they worked, all the while having regrets that I had had the idea in the first place of modernising the heating system. Then there were the nights. I would wake up in the early hours, naggingly curious as to whether the heaters were operating; and I would lie wondering, trying to make up my mind whether I had the energy to satisfy my curiosity. At last I would clamber out of bed.

'I'm going to have a look at the heaters,' I murmured one

early morning to Jeannie.

Half an hour later I returned.

'How were they?'

'Number three was out.'

'What did you do?'

'Kicked it.'

'Did that help?'

'No . . . it's still out.'

My exasperation was driving me to childish demonstration.

The manufactureres, however, were helpful. They despatched an expert from their base at Watford who declared on arrival that similar heaters were operating amiably all over the country.

'The same model?'

'Exactly the same model,' he replied.

I felt, at this moment, that he was thinking that I had invented the misdeeds of the heaters. His firm had an impeccable reputation. If, therefore, the model had proved itself elsewhere there was no possible logical reason why it shouldn't be equally successful at Minack.

'Well,' I said boisterously, forcing a joke, 'the pixies must have got at them.'

A part of the heaters had to be re-designed in the end; and then the heaters began to operate normally. Eight weeks after their installation they were at last looking after our tomato plants automatically. Thereupon the thermostats broke down. They went mad. Sometimes they pushed the heat up to 90 degrees when it should have been 60 degrees; sometimes it went to 20 degrees. They too were changed by the manufacturers who now shared my opinion that we all would have been better off if we had never heard of each other.

On one of my excursions to look at the heaters I had become acquainted with a rabbit that appeared to suffer from an obsession to have its young in number three mobile.

Every night for a month if had been digging a hole under the rail upon which the mobile rested; and every morning I had blocked it up, only for the rabbit to dig another hole as soon as darkness fell. Once inside, the rabbit excavated a burrow with such speed that by morning the burrow was seven or eight feet long and three feet deep at the far end; and here also was the nest of dried grass and peat. This nightly activity could not be expected to help the growth of the tomato plants. True the rabbit avoided digging up the plants themselves, but the burrow played havoc with the roots; and there was always the threat that one morning I might find the young in the nest.

I was advised to set a snare. Snares have taken the place of the now illegal gin traps, and I regret to say that they are a necessity where rabbits have become too plentiful again after myxamatosis. Rabbits used to cry out in the fields around us when they were caught in a gin trap, then they waited until the morning before the trapper arrived to kill them. The snare catches the wretched rabbit; and provided the snare is set at the entrance of a rabbit hole no other animal is likely to be harmed. Unhappily the law allows the snare to be set at random in the fields. This can mean a prowling cat can be caught. I have never known this happen but the possibility exists; and so when snares are in the neighbourhood, Lama is never out of sight. I believe the most humane way of dealing with rabbits is by the use of nets and a ferret. The net straddles a warren and the ferret drives them into it where they are quickly killed by the hunter. Gas, pumped into the hole of an otherwise sealed warren, is often used. I once saw this about to happen at a spot where I knew badgers occupied the underground chambers, not rabbits. I raced across a field towards the men who were in charge, shouting at the top of my voice, and was half a minute too late. They were looking the other way. They sent a whiff of cyanide gas into a hole; and for weeks afterwards Jeannie and I were waiting to see badger tracks in the area again. We saw tracks *coming* to the sealed sett. It was six months before we saw the sett had been opened up again. It was meagre satisfaction that I had screamed at the men when I reached them. One badger more or less was not going to affect their sleep at night.

I would not set a snare for my rabbit at any price. I had, in any case, become involved in its struggle for a home.

Absurdly sentimental, I can hear the cynics say, and so I suppose I ought to feel ashamed; and yet I have never been able to understand why the description of a person being sentimental is derogatory, while the description of a person being cynical denotes a certain superiority. The sentimental are at least trying to be kind, the cynical on the other hand are trying to find a way of proving themselves by doubting the value of sincerity. As I have found that truth is always changing, I am also aware that I can, at one moment, be sentimental, and at another a cynic; but I have no doubt that, of the two roles, I prefer myself when I am sentimental.

I had destroyed the burrow many times, and the rabbit still persisted with its intention to have its young in the mobile. Surely, I argued, it would come to its senses when it realised my determination. There were normal burrows galore. Why not give up the futile battle against myself? The burrow filled in, the nest destroyed, the hole under the rail blocked up . . . all this night after night. Any sensible rabbit ought to have realised it couldn't win.

Then I met the rabbit face to face.

It was early morning and I was half asleep, and I had dragged myself from my bed to satisfy my neurotic curiosity about the heaters. Dawn was just breaking and the sky was already reflecting light although the sun had not yet risen. An owl hooted from the wood on my left, and out to sea I noticed the starboard light of a fishing boat bound for Newlyn. I walked barefooted across the grass wet with dew, and reached the mobile number three, and began to walk along the side of it keeping a look out for the spot where the rabbit had made its nightly entrance. I found it at the far end this time, adjacent to the sliding door; and I looked around for a stone with which to block it up, found one, and proceeded to bend down to put it into position.

As I did so I found myself at nose level with the rabbit. It had come round the corner of the mobile at a pace, and it had stopped at the sight of me with its forelegs in front, like a racehorse refusing at a fence. And its mouth was stuffed with dried grass.

It never came to the mobile again. The fright brought

sense to it. No doubt it found a nice burrow among those on the other side of the hedge to the field; and its young were probably among those who later on in the summer ate our carrots. My own last sight of her was as she raced away from me across the field, her mouth still stuffed with dried grass; and as she disappeared the sun was rising behind Porthleven across the bay, and the dawn chorus had begun to sing around me.

Others were interested in our tomatoes; blackbirds, for instance, relished them, and when I opened up the vents in the morning before Geoffrey arrived I could spot certain blackbirds who were impatiently waiting for me. There were, this summer, a couple of males with bright yellow beaks who kept watch for me in the willow trees; and there were a female or two who perched patiently on the mobiles. As soon as I had pulled down the lever and the vents rose skywards, I would observe these characters pause for a second, then disappear through the opening; and I would know they were hurrying to their breakfast. At all times of the day a blackbird would be in one greenhouse or another; and in the evening when I closed down the vents I had to be careful to see that I didn't catch a blackbird as it came out of the greenhouse through one of them; but we did at any rate find a way of minimising the damage they did.

We left the tomatoes they had pecked where they had found them, whether on a stem or on the ground, and the blackbirds went on pecking them before they started on a fresh one. This was considerate on their part. The tomatoes they demolished were not therefore so many in the long run; and anyhow Jeannie believed that a lost tomato was cheap payment for a blackbird's song.

Boris also liked tomatoes. In fact he liked them so much that he appeared to behave as if he were a connoisseur of tomatoes. He was fussy about each one he selected, and he was not so co-operative as the blackbirds. He preferred to waddle along a row biting a piece out of one tomato then another as, in another sphere, an experienced wine taster sips importantly a range of wines. Boris never finished, as the blackbirds did, a tomato he had once tasted; and so he was a menace when the first truss was ripening because the tomatoes were easily within his reach. Thus he had to be prevented from entering the greenhouse; and the greenhouse concerned was the one in front of the cottage, the others being too far away from his normal perambulations.

It might appear that it was easy for us to stop him, and indeed it was; all we had to do was to block the lower part of the open doors, the doors we kept open on warm summer days to help ventilation, with the two wire-framed trays that we had nearby for the purpose. Unfortunately we were always forgetting to use them. Time and again there would be a cry from one of us: 'Boris is eating the tomatoes . . . nobody has put the trays across the doors.' Then one of us would go in and tell him that he had to leave; and he would hiss and waggle his tail feathers, and slowly plod outside. Later in the season, when the trusses were out of his reach, we did not have to disturb him if he chose to spend the day in the greenhouse; and sometimes Lama would be there too. Lama curled up in a small black ball, Boris with his head tucked inside his wing. Both sound asleep.

Incidents like these filled our summer days, trivial moments of diversion, the minutiae of living. I would sit on the bridge, staring across the shallow valley, the sea to my right, listening to the sounds that belonged to these summer days . . . pigeons cooing in the wood, a lark singing, a cuckoo in the distance, the flap of waves on rocks, a girl's voice calling in the cows, the chugging engine of a fishing boat, the donkeys' snorting. Yet unimportant in themselves these passing pleasures posed the question, the everlasting question of the twentieth century . . . has anyone the right to slow down the tempo of his life in an attempt to come to terms with his inner self? Or should he surrender to the pressure of conventional living, accept the tribal customs, sacrifice truth in the pursuit of power, view life as if from an express train?

Most of us conform. We stifle the secret hopes we have for personal freedom but find we cannot kill them. They were with us before we were smoothed by habit; and though sometimes they seem to fade away as the years pass, we suddenly find ourselves faced with them again in the form of frustration. There they are, challenging our weak selves, demanding why we have betrayed them.

Expediency, we reply, we had to earn a living. We became involved in a career, and we were chained to its progress. Or we may be practical by explaining that we never had the capital, never could hope to acrue the capital, that would have made it possible for us to break the pattern of our lives. Or we may admit that we lazily allowed time to slip by. Or we may say that the chance for change never came our way, or perhaps we didn't have the wit to recognise it when it was there.

Yet whatever the reason the middle-aged of today have an excuse if they believe they have failed themselves. They were caught unawares by the great god efficiency which is the deity of progress. They were passively passing their lives away, vaguely expecting their dreams to be fulfilled in some distant future, when suddenly they were forced to worship this new god; and this god, uncontrolled by any humanitarian definition as to what he should give in return for the upsets he causes, decrees the closing down of old established businesses, orders victims of takeovers to look for jobs elsewhere, force homes to be sold as a consequence, children to be removed from their schools, and the lives of people to be disrupted at any age when they might expect to be consolidating. The efficiency cult can become the human tragedy of the seventies. It is obsessed with the cutting of costs. Nothing else matters; and so quality suffers, and service, and the dignity of individuals.

The young, some of them, are alert to what faces them. They are moving into an age which has no precedent in British history. For there has been no war to decimate a generation as in 1914 and 1939; and so there will be a larger supply of young brains and energy competing for key jobs than ever before. There will be relays of such young brains; and the god efficiency will exploit them. Thus clever minds will be squeezed dry, physical stamina exhausted, in the service of combines and governments because fresh replacements will always be waiting in reserve; and brilliant men, so occupied by the immediate problems of the day that they have no time to keep up to date with contemporary research, will suddenly find themselves discarded for being old fashioned; full of promise at thirty, unwanted at forty.

There will be no place for the mediocre, or for the dreamers, or for those whose talents do not blossom in the examination room, or for those whose minds develop late. Fail a paper by five marks and they will be blackballed for ever in the career they want to follow . . . a dead-end by the age of twenty-one, smarting from a failure they believe to be unfair, a disappointment to their parents, frustrated with life before it has really begun. No wonder the seeds of revolt germinate. What has society to offer youth in such circumstances? The shallow compensations may await, but these provide no basic satisfaction to the inner self. An inflationary wage for unskilled work does not help to bring peace of mind if there is no pride or pleasure in doing it; or if it offers no future except to grow old as a unit in a computer, electronics giving orders for ever. So when youth rebels today, he is in fact rebelling against the prospect of his organised future; for he too is wanting personal freedom. The middle-aged may disapprove of his tactics, but the aim is shared. Both seek to own their souls.

Meanwhile the middle-aged faced the present. Those who have been successful, the ambitious and the power hungry, chase the prizes which beckon them, then find the prizes have turned to ashes when they have been won. Material ostentation, making people jump to obey their whims, living a jet existence around the world, creates a spiritual vacuum, or ill health, or a broken home. Speed has destroyed quiet moments of reflection by offering the successful too many alternatives, too many opportunities. A safety valve is missing. They have no time to contemplate, are scared to do so. Then suddenly the party is over, and they are lost.

The others, the undistinguished and the unimportant, always loyal to their families, leading their conventional lives out of a sense of duty, watch the prices go up, the fares go up, and then are forced to sacrifice another small pleasure which had helped to compensate for the queuing, the sardine travelling, and the noise which dulls the senses. They fear the change which is taking place around them, but are mute. This is progress for the common good so it is useless to protest. They gaze at the monster earth-moving machines clawing at the ground, and watch buildings familiar as old friends disappear into lorry loads of rubble. Nothing is secure. The fields where the Sunday walk is taken are scheduled to be the site of the new housing estate. The road in front of the house is to be widened, and it will demolish the front garden. Only the insensitive can be the winners. Only those who, in the name of efficiency, dictate the orders. And perhaps even they may sometimes wonder whether their own lives have become victims of their own actions.

Yet these forces of material progress will be moving even more quickly. There are no logical reasons to stop them. We have to accept the fact that, because of the population explosion, because of the trends existing today, the rights of the individual will become increasingly subservient to the demands of the community. So what can anyone do to shake himself free?

Conventions have always been the enemy of individualism, the herd always ridicules the odd man out. But today it is even more difficult to be the odd man out because regulations have been devised to control him. He cannot, as I did once, wake up one morning and decide to live in the country and live on virtually nothing.

The time was during the last few weeks of summer before war broke out. I had returned from a year of travelling round the world, and I was offered a derelict cottage near Truro where I began to write a book about my travels. I was alone, and free, and thankful I was able to live the life I wanted. Nobody was ready to interfere with me provided I obeyed the law; and the law, then, wasn't too complicated to obey. Nor did I have to be registered, except for my birth certificate, with any of the government departments of the day. No self-employed National Insurance stamps to find money for. I was totally free except for my personal doubts.

I have chased the mood of that time ever since; and another time, a few months before, when I lived on an island called Toopua two hundred miles away from Tahiti. Then, without communication with the outside world, finding myself so close to nature that I looked upon myself as a stranger, part of a community who were so natural in their behaviour and so untainted by western influence that they were effortlessly happy, I promised myself that after my return to England I would immediately make plans to live for a long while on the island. Needless to say I never did go back. Needless to say that the time came when Toopua was bulldozed into an airstrip, providing western civilisation with another triumphant example of progress; and it then became, like the other islands of the South Seas, a tourist centre for the trivial. And instead of Toopua, I found Minack.

Money, of course, is the bogey, however fervent the desire, however mature the determination to be free. When Jeannie and I came to Minack our weekly expenses were £3 a week. But if anyone today wants to break away from his customary environment, he has to act with a banker's common sense. That's the bore. He can't act rashly, impulsively like Jeannie and I did. He has to calculate, and in the course of calculating, enthusiasm is inclined to dim; and so no change is made in the end.

It is, however, easier to feel free in the country; and cheaper. In a city there are too many diversions which give people the illusion of participating in real living, when in fact they are watching as outsiders. To feel free, in the sense that you become aware that you were born to belong to yourself and not to a Fuhrer, you have to possess certain traits of the hermit; and it is simpler to be a hermit in the country than in the city. You do not have to pretend. You do not have to spend money on non-essentials in order to keep up appearances. Clothes can be old. Vegetables are the cost of the seed. Blackberries stock you with jam for the year. You can brew your own wine, make your own bread, grow your own tobacco for that matter. And you will find yourself re-adjusting your ideas as to what constitutes wealth. Getting up in the morning without hurrying is worth a good deal. So too that you have no traffic jams to join. So too that you can stand and stare without appointments to keep. So too that there is no neighbour's radio to annoy you. So too that you can look up into a silent sky. All these are put on the credit side when you calculate the cost of changing your life.

For although we are living in the affluent age, a peasant's way of life is coming into its own again. Basic goods are becoming luxuries, and so those who can learn to be self-supporting will be the lucky ones. This return to simplicity is the only practical method that any one with limited funds can follow; and yet it is so easy to say this, so difficult to put into practice. I sometimes think of the succession of crofters who lived at Minack over the past five hundred years, and envy them. They did not have to compromise as Jeannie and I have to compromise. Sometimes I touch the old rocks around the cottage which they also touched, and the years run away in my mind, and I feel close to these people whose lives were governed by the seasons. Then they believed God was in charge, not governments. They had a natural faith. Simplicity was an uncomplicated virtue taken for granted. Wisdom was instinctive, not a product of theory. Nature crushed them, and exalted them; and they were a part of the world around them as the hares, and the corn, and the wild seas, and badgers on moonlit nights, and the cries of vixen, and haywains, and the swallows coming in the spring.

Jeannie and I are aware that we possess what constitutes the new kind of wealth. Seldom passes the day during which one of us does not exclaim to the other that the life we lead is the happiest that we could imagine, and small things will prompt us to exclaim this. The sight of a Red Admiral butterfly on the feathery white flowers of a privet, bees roaming the escallonia, the croak of a frog in a hole in one of the stone walls, a dunnock feeding its young, the first whiff of the mignonette scent on the bridge, the Mediterranean blue of the sea. And yet we have to compromise.

We have to perform sophisticated tasks in order to preserve the basic simplicity which we love, because there is an inevitable conflict between our work on the land and the results of my books about Minack. Neither would exist without the other, but the books have taken us away from the hard slog which used to be our daily routine. Perhaps this is just as well. Yet we sometimes look back with nostalgia to the days when nothing else filled our minds except the earthy task in hand.

Nestlings were now in the nest in the barn, and the parents were skimming the stable meadow, soaring into the sky, snatching the invisible flies, then swooping down and darting through the doorway of the barn. No lavish spectacle devised by man could offer greater pleasure. A summer's day, green bracken covering the moorland across the valley, foxgloves pointing pink arms to the sky, the white plates of the elderberry flowers, carpets of buttercups in the donkey field with the donkeys lying outstretched among them.

We had finished packing the tomatoes around midday, and Geoffrey had gone off in the car to Penzance to take them to the wholesaler close to the harbour. Jeannie, meanwhile, had disappeared into the cottage to be with Emily, Geoffrey's young wife, who was helping with the cleaning; and there was I on the bridge when I heard the sound of a car's wheels on the gravel way up the lane.

At first I thought it was an ordinary visitor. Then suddenly I realised it was travelling very fast; and when it reached the turning before Monty's Leap the driver started tooting his horn. The car had reached the Leap before I saw who it was; and it was my friend Jack from the farm at the top. I could not for the life of me understand why he was driving so fast. In a second I knew.

Geoffrey's house was on fire. The house he had spent years building himself in the valley on the way to St Buryan.

I hurried into the cottage to collect Emily.

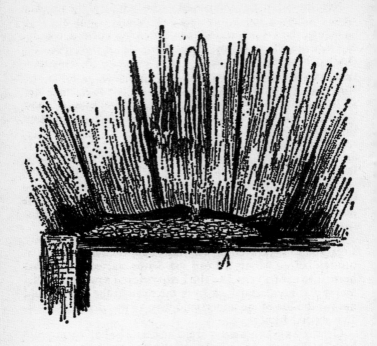

NINE

I saw the smoke billowing in the valley to my right as we
passed the Merry Maidens, that circle of stones which represent, according to legend, nineteen girls caught dancing
on a Sunday. I saw the smoke whenever the hedge was low
or there was the gap of a gateway; and I knew for certain that
this was a bad fire, because the smoke was black and thick
and in command.

'It will be all right,' I said to Jeannie and Emily beside me
in the Land Rover, 'I can't see any flames. The fire engines
must be there and damping it down.'

One tells lies on these occasions. I wonder sometimes
whether one tells them out of tact, or out of cowardice.

'Oh my home, my home,' I heard Emily crying.

We turned right at Boskenna Cross, and I put my foot down on the accelerator; and I wondered where Geoffrey might be. His habit was first to drive the Cortina with its load of tomato chips to Jennings Street where he was greeted by Fred Galley, the foreman of our wholesalers; and then park the car somewhere along the front where he ate his lunch from the pack Emily had provided. Both Jack and Bill, the farmers at the top of the hill from Minack were, I knew, trying to trace him by telephone. He had, however, another journey to do . . . he had to drive to Long Rock just outside Penzance to collect a fresh supply of tomato boxes. If he was caught at Jennings Street, he would be back within twenty minutes; if he was missed there because he had already departed for Long Rock he might be back within thirty minutes. If he had lunch between assignments he would not be back for an hour. At the moment we arrived at the fire, Geoffrey was munching his sandwiches on the front unaware that his home was being destroyed.

We joined the spectators, and spectators we could only be. There was nothing to do except watch; and when the watching became too emotional for Emily, friends took her to one of the council houses on the main road, and Jeannie went off to fetch her mother from her home two or three miles away. The fire had started in the adjoining house. The occupant had left for Penzance in his van around midday, and ten minutes later Geoffrey's mother, who lived a stone's throw away, saw smoke coming out of the porch. She ran up the hill to the road to give the alarm. There was a team of County Council workmen at work on the roadway, and while one rushed off to telephone the fire brigade, the others ran down the four hundred yards of track to Geoffrey's house. It was useless for them to try to put out the blaze, so they proceeded frantically to bring out as much of the furniture as possible; and when we arrived the grass field above the house was witness to their courage, for lying there at random was a bed, and an electric cooker, and a gramophone, and numerous other household belongings. But the bulk, including all the clothes, was still in the house; and though the firemen were doing their best, the flames, fanned by a south-westerly wind, were sweeping through the rooms;

and the glass of the great window which looked across the countryside to the Ding Dong country in the distance had already been broken into a thousand fragments by the heat. We all just stood and stared and muttered to each other our theories as to how it had begun; and I remember seeing Geoffrey's mother, a fine character who has always seemed to me to represent the best in country life, sitting on a rock, looking with resignation at the flames eating away the roof of this house which she had watched her son build with the aid of his father, a craftsman carpenter. The adjoining house was now a smoking shell; and all the fury of the flames were concentrated on Geoffrey's house. And there was still no sign of Geoffrey.

Fires hypnotise. People will stand staring at the flames snaking through rooms, watch timbers fall and walls collapse, gaze at the helmeted firemen training their jets of water through broken windows, like rabbits dazed by car headlights. This behaviour is not caused by a macabre pleasure. It is the awesome sight of an element let loose which seems alive in its viciousness. The first big fire I ever witnessed was in the Ancoats district of Manchester, and I had been sent to cover the story for the *Daily Express* by my news editor. It was night, and the building concerned was a ten-storey warehouse, and when I arrived it was already an inferno. I was fascinated into inaction. I stood staring up at the flames which were quite out of control. I saw a vast side of the building totter, then crash to the ground. I forgot why I was there. I was so hypnotised by the sight of it all that it never occurred to me that I had a job to do. Some two hours after my arrival I felt a tap on my shoulder. A senior colleague had arrived. 'I've been sent,' he remarked gently, 'to find out if you are alive.'

I did not, however, on this occasion stay gazing at the fire. I wanted to be on the main road when Geoffrey arrived, and I was up there talking to the officer in charge of the fire tender when I caught sight of the Cortina; and in a flash it had reached us and drawn up at the kerb. There is nothing one can do in such circumstances except to hold out a hand and convey sympathy by silence. He was calmer than I could have ever been.

'Everything has gone, hasn't it?' and he spoke as if he did not want an answer.

The generous village of St Buryan immediately came to their help. A home was offered to them and the two children, Philip and Julie, so that the family would not have to be separated; and clothes were showered on them, and toys. But as far as Geoffrey himself was concerned, I knew his calmness was only bottling up his emotions. Every inch of that house he knew intimately. Every nail, screw, floorboard, beam, slate, breeze block, and polished refinement he had planned with his father, and bought, and installed . . . and now they were a charred mess. Two years after the house had been completed it had become a shell for no fault of his own. An experience which might make anyone feel bitter.

I let him be on the Saturday, then went over on the Sunday morning. I walked down from the road, unpleasantly aware of the acrid smell coming from the desolation, and could see no one. Then I passed along the slope beyond the entrance to the house, and found two silent figures poking in the debris outside that great window which looked upon the distant Ding Dong country. Geoffrey and his father were picking up broken glass, and as I murmured my condolences I quickly realised that my tone may have been appreciated, they were not requiring any pity. They possessed the fatalistic outlook of the countryman, and this fire was part of the pattern of droughts, and storms, and ruined crops and lost harvests. The disaster had occurred, and it was no use to sit back and do nothing but moan about it. And so I found they were already planning the rebuilding of the house, and looking forward to the day when it would he a home again.

There was a fire at Minack many years ago, and there is a dark line along the granite lintel above the fireplace where a blazing beam left its mark. I have asked octogenarians in the neighbourhood whether they remember the occasion, and their replies are vague. Minack was a far away place which few people from St Burayn ever visited. The full name for the cottage is Dominack, but it has always been called Minack, pronounced Mynack, by those born and bred in the St Buryan and Lamorna area. In the neighbouring

89

parish of St Leven is the Minack Rock from which the famous cliff theatre takes its name. This Minack, however, is pronounced Minnack. Hence when I have talked to old people about the fire, they have replied: 'I think blind Trewern was down Minack that time.' Or: 'I don't remember. I've never been down Minack in my life.' But it seems that the fire took place just before the first world war or perhaps shortly after it started. The cottage was thatched in those days. Jeannie and I have often said that we would like to have it thatched again; and I once asked a thatcher how much this would cost. The price, I suppose, was not really excessive, but the thatcher, a formidable personality, laid down a condition that we could not accept. He insisted that the work would take three months, and during that period he would have to live in his caravan close to the cottage.

At the time of the fire there were upstairs rooms. The black line along the lintel is on the same level as the ledge which surrounds the living room, proving that this was the ceiling level; and if the ceiling existed today at that level I would always be stooping. Nor could there have been much space between the floor side of the ceiling and the roof. Thatch has to be very steep or the reeds become a bog after rain; and so the upstairs rooms, closed in by the thatch climbing to the massive, granite chimney must have been tiny. And where did the reeds come from which provided the thatch? There is an area of land sloping steeply down to the sea between the Minack boundary and the jagged point of Carn Barges in which reeds grow. They are not the type which thatchers use today, but there is little doubt that they were used in the past; and so the reeds I see when I walk to Carn Barges with the donkeys are the same stock which may have thatched Minack for centuries.

Geoffrey was back on Monday. By half past eight he had filled a couple of large baskets with tomatoes and he said to me that the morning's picking would amount to over five hundredweight. He always had an instinctive knowledge as to how much he would pick, and he was seldom wrong. It was the instinct of someone who was interested in his job, the result of enthusiasm he had shown for the plants all though their growing time. I went back into the cottage and told Jeannie. We liked to have an estimate of the quantity of tomatoes to be picked; we then could gauge how long the grading, weighing and packing would take. We decided on this occasion that if we were not interrupted we would finish by midday, and the tomatoes would reach the wholesalers before they closed for lunch. By eleven o'clock we were well up to schedule, and I was happily remarking upon this to Jeannie when I heard a car coming down the lane, then draw up outside the cottage. 'Hell,' I said, and went off to see who it was, passing Boris on the way, head tucked under his wing, squatting asleep on the London Pride which edged the rose garden. I reached the car, saw there was only one occupant, and immediately guessed he was a Government official. I observed that he had that purposeful but remote manner which always puts me on my guard. I greeted him suspiciously.

'Good morning,' I said.

'I'm from the Training Board,' he replied, 'you asked me to call.'

Indeed I had. A few weeks before, the newly constituted Agricultural, Horticultural and Forestry Training Board had summoned me for failing to pay the annual levy. The levy was £3 for each person employed; and as there was only Geoffrey to pay for, it might seem churlish that I had withheld the money. I was, however, one among thousands of growers and farmers who had failed to pay. We believed the Board was out of touch with reality, and so we made this gesture of protest against those in far away offices who devise ill-conceived regulations.

Horticulture is so different from the car, steel, and any other industry; and yet the theory boys had put it in the same category. The heavy industries are concentrated in large areas, the horticultural industry is splintered in small units all over the country; and while the heavy industries deal with mass production, the horticultural industry growing a multitude of different crops and facing all the vagaries of nature, has to deal with each problem individually.

Thus staff training is a commonsense affair; and everyone, boss or employee, has to continue his training throughout his working life. Every day you learn something from your practical work. Every day there is a new problem to face, a result of unusual weather, an unexpected pest, a mysterious plant disease. There is very little which is rational in horticulture. You cannot even organise the marketing because it depends on climatic conditions which are uncontrollable; and when expenses rise you cannot even put up your prices because you are governed by the wholesale market to which you send your produce. Horticulture does not need theoretical training schemes. It already has practical methods of helping itself. If a grower, for instance, needs specialist help he can visit one of the well-organised Government sponsored horticultural stations, or receive personal visits from helpful members of the National Advisory Service. For new recruits to the industry there are various Institutes and Colleges which teach the basic knowledge. You would say, therefore, that horticulture was well enough served by instructional opportunities. The theory boys think otherwise. Here are two extracts from their leaflets:

'It is advisable to teach an employee to teach instructional techniques to key workers who can then instruct others at their place of work.'

'Instructor training can provide the following benefits to the employer. Organised training on his own holding, tailored to meet the employee's need, an opportunity to follow without difficulty his employee's progress and capability. The instructing employee normally enjoys increased prestige and job satisfaction.' Sheer verbiage.

Nevertheless I decided to change my tactics after the summons had been served. I would challenge the Board's usefulness. I would pay the levy, then seek the Board's advice. I would behave as a reasonable employer, anxious to take advantage of Government paternalism, eager to look for ways of improving Geoffrey's horticultural techniques. I would discover at first hand how the Training Board operated; and hence my request that an official should call on me. What horticultural education would he suggest?

Jeannie said afterwards that when she saw me disappear

92

with the official into my office she waited for raised voices. She is, in a way, more impatient than I am, more quickly aroused by injustice, personal or social, real or imaginary; and she will sometimes want to go on the attack while I am advising caution. On the other hand I have a quick temper when caught off guard, and then I rush into an argument with fury. If, however, I have had time to contemplate upon what has vexed me, I attack with stealth. This, for me, is one of the advantages of not possessing a telephone. I can seldom be surprised. The irritations usually come by post; and I have to reply to them by post.

The irritation, on this occasion, had arrived, however, without warning; for although I had asked to see the official, he had in fact caught me by surprise. And so Jeannie was correct in thinking she might hear raised voices when he and I were alone in my office. My quick temper might dominate, and I was aware that I would let it do so if the man gave me half a chance.

He didn't. Instead of adopting the official tone of superiority I had expected, the man was disarming. I found myself feeling like a boxer who, all ready for a fight, sees his opponent throw in the towel before the first round begins. He agreed with the points I made about the Training Board instead of contesting them. He agreed that the Rosewarne Experimental Station at Camborne was one of the finest horticultural stations in the country; and that visits to see the practical work done there during the course of the year was the best possible educational value. He agreed that this area was served from Truro by highly efficient advisers from the Ministry of Agriculture National Advisory Service. He agreed that the Training Board could not offer any better training opportunities. So why should I pay a levy?

The official left without providing the answer; and I went back to Jeannie to help her finish the tomatoes.

'You seem deflated,' she said.

'I am.'

'Why? Didn't he annoy you?'

'He was far too nice.'

'What a shame,' she said laughing.

'But he left me with something to think about.'

'What exactly?'

'Well, it's an old story which only comes alive when it happens to yourself, I mean being a victim of the bureaucratic machine, and there are thousand upon thousand like me. Not just in this Training Board business, but in dozens of other different spheres. A decision is made in a wall carpeted room in Whitehall, and the man who has made it goes out and has a good lunch, walks around St James's Park, feeds the ducks, goes back to his office and already the consequences of the morning decision has been set in motion which leads in the end to the victims being angry when they first hear about it, then frightened, then resigned when they realise they cannot do anything about it.'

'Protest campaigns often succeed.'

'Only if the protesters have power to blackmail. The rest of us are ignored, we have to be obedient. We can bleat as much as we like but we will be forced to accept the decision however foolish it may be.'

'I just don't agree,' said Jeannie, she was weighing the last chip of tomatoes, 'time and time again ordinary people have made their views felt so strongly that decisions have been changed. Remember Alan Herbert saying to us long ago that people must always protest whenever their genuine feelings are aroused?'

'I do.'

A. P. Herbert, forerunner of those who wave banners in front of television cameras, attacked injustice and humbug with wit.

'It is a question of alerting people,' went on Jeannie, 'Alan said you must make people aware of an issue and the battle is half won.'

'He has always been an optimist.'

'You *are* cynical today,' said Jeannie, 'it seems to me to be time for lunch.'

I stapled the card on the last chip, and stacked the chip along with the others, all sixty of them.

'The man insisted that I will still have to go on paying the levy,' I said.

'If everyone continues to protest,' Jeannie answered

cheerfully, 'the law will be changed.' It has been; but not before I was summoned again for non-payment of a second levy.

The wind had shifted to the south, and although the weather was still warm and gentle I felt rain was not far away. I went into the cottage and poured each of us a glass of wine, then went ahead of Jeannie to the bridge. It was pleasant and sheltered enough there to sit down on the wooden bench, and stare, and eat the sandwiches which Jeannie brought to me a few minutes later.

'I saw Daisy this morning,' Jeannie said. Daisy, the little grey cat, mother of Lama.

'That's strange,' I answered, 'we seldom see her until the afternoon.'

We had often observed that she never appeared in the morning. She made her sedate way along her regular route any time from noon onwards, although over the years I remember several exceptions. There was a very cold winter, snow feet deep over our daffodil meadows in early March; and one morning I saw these paw prints on the way to the onion meadow, then caught sight of Daisy just ahead of me. Daisy was too much a part of nature ever to be unduly concerned by the contrariness of the weather. It was a part of her life, like the scent of the daffodils in the meadows in which she wandered, like the hot soil she stepped on after cliff potatoes had been dug in blazing summers, like the gales she hid from, behind lichen covered granite hedges. Strange that a cat one never touched should become so familiar.

'Heavens,' I said suddenly, 'the swallows are dive-bombing Boris!'

The bridge seems to breed inconsequential remarks. No discipline in the conversation is needed in order to have pleasure. One is watching a passing scene, and this warrants interruptions, or sudden changes of subject; a sudden flight of birds across the sky, a cuckoo calling urgently in the wood, Lama stalking a mouse in the grass by the apple tree, scores of such incidents are considered by ourselves as moments of importance. So now with Boris. Boris attacked by the swallows! The old boy was wagging his tail feathers

95

in embarrassment. He had been up to the cottage for a meal of crumbled homemade bread scattered in front of the door by Jeannie; and he was beside the lavender bush on his way back to the grass around his pond when the attack took place.

Swish! One of the swallows missed his beak by inches. Swish! The other swallow skimmed his back. Poor Boris was bewildered.

'The young ones are soon to fly,' I said to Jeannie, then got up and went down the path to walk beside him. He plodded very slowly these days, and stiffly as if he had rheumatism. We had been more anxious than ever about him, although he gave no positive sign that he was ailing. He still had a good appetite. He still flapped happily in his pond. But there was an air about him that gave the impression of age, of a general slowing down of his ways.

'Come on old Boris,' I said, 'I'll be your escort.' He hissed fussily as he waddled on. He wanted me to know that he was perfectly capable of looking after himself.

He was, of course.

I was only showing my affection for him.

'Boris!' I suddenly shouted, 'they're dive-bombing *me*!'

A swallow had passed so close that I felt the rush of air on my face.

TEN

The flight of the young did not take place for a week. We would spy on them through the window on the lane side of the barn, pressing our faces against the glass because the dark inside made it difficult to see the nest on the ledge. Or I made a quick investigation by entering the barn itself, and looked at the nest at eye level. There were four in the brood. They would stare back at me, unafraid for a second, their heads rimming the nest, a line of fledgling white along their tiny beaks, incongruously reminding me of black and white minstrels. Their twittering would suddenly cease, their heads disappear, and I would then hurry away before a parent discovered me.

The parents, meanwhile, continued to dive-bomb the inhabitants of Minack. No one was spared their attention. Lama, Jeannie, Geoffrey, Fred and Penny, the gulls on the roof, jackdaws, woodpeckers, magpies, crows, all were to share the experience of Boris. Jackdaws, magpies and crows deserved any rough treatment they might receive; but not the rest of us. Indeed I began to wonder whether the object of the dive-bombing *was* to attack. No one was threatening the young, safe inside the barn, not even the jackdaws, magpies and crows. So were the antics perhaps a form of celebration? Were they a young swallow couple rejoicing in their achievement of producing the first brood of their lives? Were they, by their daredevil flights, trying to share the pleasure of their good fortune? If so, the response from the inhabitants of Minack must have proved disappointing.

Lama, for instance, did not find it amusing. She liked on a summer's morning to stroll towards Monty's Leap, taking her time, alert for any rustle in the grass, sniffing sweet scents, until she reached the stream where she leisurely partook of the water. The essence of this ritual was the way she could carry it out undisturbed. I would not have dared to interrupt her while the stroll was in progress; and I feel sure that if a stranger driving a car had seen her in the lane ahead of him, he would not just have stopped the car. He would have backed it out of sight. It was so perfectly obvious that she was communing with her soul, and had at all costs to be left alone.

The swallows, however, did not get the message. They observed the black plush creature below them, and thought what a delightful gesture it would be if they acknowledged her presence by slipping past her whiskers at speed. I happened to be watching Lama the first time the gesture was made; and she had momentarily paused by the elderberry tree beside which was a small syringa bush. Both were in flower and the scents clearly delighted her. She had her face up-turned to a white bloom on the syringa when a swallow dived from behind her, skimming both her nose and the white bloom, and forcing her to leap round automatically in cat-like defensive reaction. Her fury was increased by her failure to spot the enemy. Only myself was in sight, and I was certainly too far away to have been the offender. So she looked foolish; and was obviously very annoyed. Then, after a minute or two's pause, after a courageous and successful effort to subdue her annoyance, she set off again towards Monty's Leap.

She had reached the small, unused well at the side of the lane a few yards further on, when the swallow did it again. He whistled past her tail. She was at that moment totally absorbed by some activity inside the well, and I suspected she had heard a frog croaking within it. It is a shallow well, prettily placed beneath a great rock with a slab of stone overing the top of its entrance. It is a collector of land water and so it dries up in early summer, and then it becomes a comfortable hiding place for a frog or two. In spring it echoes with frog songs all day long; and when Jane and Shelagh were with us, when we used to bunch and pack our flowers in the old stables which is almost opposite, we used to play a game giving words to the croaking songs.

Lama never noticed this swoop on her tail. Her one-track mind was intent on the well, and she crouched beside it, head alert, and she seemed to me that she was about to leap inside it. Then, just as suddenly as the mystery sound had caught her attention, she lost interest; and the stroll was on again, a casual sauntering stroll denoting a cat who was at peace with the world.

The swallow, of course, was observing her. I could see him gambolling in the sky, high above the elms, then across the stable meadow and over the old hut where we used to shoot potato seed, then behind the cottage and up to the well. Then he turned, and like an aircraft lining up for a bomb attack, he swept over the bridge down the path which joined the lane, diving lower and lower, faster and faster, until with perfect timing he brushed the two little black ears of the lady who was so benignly enjoying her morning.

This time she did not ignore what had happened. She saw the swallow flash over the Leap a few yards ahead; and then belatedly displayed her displeasure. The swallow did not witness it. He was high up in the sky by then, and out of sight; and anyhow no harm would have come to him if he had. Lama's only weapon was a snarl, a turned-up lip, an ugly face. It might have scared a mouse, but not a swallow.

99

The jackdaws, magpies and crows were unperturbed by a swallow attack, for they were born to expect to be hated. The green woodpecker dipping its way up the valley to the wood was, however, surprised that any swallow should give him attention; and he laughed in apparent nervousness. It is an uncanny sound the woodpecker's laugh, for it is gay yet sad; and I have listened to it sometimes and wondered fancifully whether it represents the laughter of someone who died when they were young. Such a thought is too romantic; but the truth remains that a woodpecker's laugh makes me remember sometimes those I have known.

The gulls objected strongly to the swallows' behaviour. They considered the attitude of the swallows so impertinent that they would point their beaks to the sky as they stood on the flat top of the chimney or on the rim of the roof, and cry out their views on the subject. All through the year they were accustomed to treat the chimney and roof as their home during the day; and to expect their measured flight to the rocks and back to be undisturbed. Then these upstarts from South Africa who basked in the sun all those months when they themselves coped with the rain and the gales, suddenly started to bait them. It was intolerable. Yet they were powerless to stop the baiting. The swallows would skim over them as they cried, or dart at them as they glided towards the sea. It was easy to realise that the swallows infuriated them; but I have also to be fair to the swallows. The gulls are solemn creatures. I have never thought they had much sense of humour.

The donkeys, however, were very tolerant. They were banned from entering the barn, but they were not banned from the small paddock outside. The barn wall facing this small paddock caught the sun in the early morning, and its warmth often lured the donkeys to stand alongside it. This meant they were adjacent to the stable door through the top half of which flew the swallows as they went to and fro feeding the young. Not unnaturally the donkeys were intrigued by this activity; and, on awakening from a doze, they would decide to brighten their lives by having a look inside. Thus the swallows, having spent five minutes collecting insects up in the sky, would return to the barn door, beaks filled, to find two donkey bottoms facing them; while the open half of the door through which they had to fly was half blocked by two heads with large ears, peering into the semi-darkness.

There seemed to be an understanding between the donkeys and the swallows; and although the donkeys would stamp their feet when the swallows flicked past, the showed no other signs of surprise. These were donkeys in docile mood. They were curious to find out what was going on in the barn, but there was no tension in their curiosity. Fred's curiosity on other occasions can become so tense that he trembles with excitement, and then he will often blare out a bellow that sounds a little hysterical; and he will usually perform this bellow galloping across the field. He is too excited to keep still.

Various incidents can prompt this excitement. If I play hide and seek with him, if I have been so cunning as to elude him and he is at a loss to know which way to go and find me, he will often set off this bellow as he races in this direction and that; and I am then so moved by this demonstration that I emerge from my hiding place, and he will rush up to me, and there is a reunion.

Fishing boats and ships will also occasionally produce a bellow. Fred keeps a keen watch on any activity on the sea along the Minack coast. He appears to know the regular fishing boats, for although you may find him looking at them you do not receive the impression that he is particularly interested. A strange vessel, and his mood is quite different. Ears alert, nostrils quivering, you can see into his mind . . . what's that strange boat doing here? Or he may become fascinated by some craft which has anchored off shore, and although it is probably there for some quite simple reason, there are sometimes exceptions. He was fascinated, for instance, one summer evening, by a fishing boat whose skipper was repeatedly blowing a klaxon horn. This was a ready made situation for query and excitement, and Fred, who was with Penny in one of the cliff meadows at the time, responded as if he were a coastguard on duty. He was quicker to realise the skipper was in trouble than I was. He started to prance up and down the meadow, paus-

101

ing every few seconds to stare out to sea; and indeed making me feel that if he had a telescope available he would have put it to use. It was a still evening, and the klaxon horn must have been heard over a wide area. So too Fred's bellow. He let out one of the loudest bellows in his repertory and it must have echoed over the water to give comfort to the distressed skipper; and it also appeared to have had an even more practical result. Within seconds I saw a distant fishing boat alter course. The combination of a klaxon horn and a donkey's bellow had alerted the crew; and soon afterwards they were towing the boat towards Newlyn.

The nautical aspect of Fred's character received a further boost more recently when the Q.E.2 passed within a mile of Minack. We knew she was coming; and we had been asked by Captain Warwick to put up some kind of signal. The wooden stake which propped up Jeannie's washing line was purloined, and a large orange tablecloth was nailed to it. The stake, now a flagpost, was then sandwiched between two boulders on the edge of a field close to the cottage; and there we waited.

We had chosen this field because the passengers aboard were being given a running commentary by the Chief Purser; and the placing of the flagpost in this field would enable the passengers to see the cottage at the same time as the orange tablecloth. We were, however, prevented from watching the approach of the Q.E.2 by the brow of a hill; and we depended upon Geoffrey to shout from a vantage point news of her coming.

Suddenly she was upon us. It was as if she had sailed out of the hill. The sight was stupendous, so unexpectedly beautiful that I found myself wanting to cheer; and this was exactly how Fred felt too. He was so excited that he literally quivered with emotion; and when the Q.E.2 sounded three deep blasts from her siren in greeting, I felt he might leap over the cliff into the sea and swim to her. Seaman Fred had come of age.

The interest of the donkeys as to what the swallows were up to in the barn never lasted very long. They would move away in to the stable field, and if it was a fine early morning and there was a rabbit or two about, they would create a diversion for themselves by giving chase to a rabbit. I have seen them chase a rabbit from one end of the stable field to the other, though they did so in harmless fashion. They were not chasing to catch the rabbit, and the rabbit knew this; so the chase was only an innocent game.

Jeannie once saw Fred chase a fox cub through the wood. We do not allow them in the wood because they have this foolish habit of gnawing bark whenever they are bored. Some people say that they gnaw the bark so as to sharpen their teeth. Whether or not this is true, the bark is still gnawed; and as a tree will die if the trunk is made bare of bark at any circular point, it is obvious that the wood had to be put out of bounds.

However at the time Jeannie watched Fred chase a cub, we had not awakened to the damage they were doing; and they were allowed to roam as they wished. It is a very small wood, a copse in fact, but they then had its freedom. In one corner Jeannie has a small cabin where she paints and draws; and where she wrote her novel *Hotel Regina*. She was there one afternoon when she saw a cub saunter past the cabin window oblivious of her presence, or the proximity of the donkeys for that matter. It appeared to be going into the inner wood when it changed its mind; and Jeannie watched it turn, then advance towards where the donkeys were standing out of sight, close to the hut where Boris lived.

Suddenly Jeannie heard a commotion, and the cub came scampering back past her window; and a few seconds later came Fred, nose to the ground like a foxhound. But instead of the tense face of the hunter, Jeannie says that Fred was obviously laughing; and that Penny, a yard or two behind, was laughing so much that she was flinging out her back legs as if she was kicking someone when, of course, there was no one to kick. The cub, a future of danger and serious chasing and narrow escapes lying ahead, hastened speedily away; and as Jeannie watched it disappear over the wall into the inner wood she wished it well, as anyone wishes a traveller well. The donkeys, now baulked by the wall, just stared across it to the uncharted world beyond. They were not frustrated. The chase had been a momentary game. They were not trying to prove anything. Life was fun for them.

It was not much for us, however, when we had to chase *them*. One would have thought there was no reason for them ever to wish to escape from their environment. Few donkeys had such space in which to wander, such variety of grass, such succulent different delicacies in the hedges. I had had a postcard from an R.A.F. man in Arabia this summer with a message for Fred. The postcard was a photograph of two donkeys laden with packs, and it came from Muscat in the Trucial States. 'These are *working* donkeys,' wrote the sender, 'Fred never had it like this! They have never seen grass.' I showed the postcard to Penny and Fred, rubbing the photograph against their soft noses. 'Now you realise how lucky you are!' I said . . . and they both promptly started to hoot.

Their escapades are only mischievous adventures; and I have learnt that Penny is usually the leader on these occasions. She is a sly one. She appears to be such a reliable matron type of donkey, she is always in the background when Fred is showing off, she seems always more slow in her movements; and yet I have several times realised that she urges Fred to commit the initial misdemeanour. Then if Fred succeeds in opening the gate or lifting the bar across a gap which I thought I had fixed securely, Penny will push past him and take the lead; and I have known her on a walk (on walks along the cliff we always take off their halters) behave so naughtily that she succeeds by some deception in slipping past us, then rush into a gallop with Fred fast behind her, and they are away in the distance before we realise what has happened. I have known them gallop up the lane in this thundering fashion. I saw them one afternoon munching the heliotrope around Monty's Leap, and I advanced slowly to capture them, murmuring friendly noises while doing so. I learnt later that their escape on this occasion was not their fault, a gate had been left open; but I would have been in any case furious when I saw them ignore my kindly approach, and set off up the lane. Within a few yards they put on the pace. There I was panting behind them, when I saw Penny's bottom disappear round the corner, Fred on her heels. This is the type of occasion when donkeys have you at their mercy. There is nothing you can do. They are up and away, and that's that. Fortunately Bill, who has one of the farms at the top of the lane, was walking down it; and he met them coming towards him at such speed that he said afterwards they would have continued to the main road a mile away and on to Penzance had he not been there to stop them.

Escape routes, however, are not always the result of a left-open gate, a bar cleverly removed from a gap, or a latch nudged by a nose. The donkeys, during the nights they spend in the open, become well acquainted with the badgers and foxes that live in the area; and when they watch them padding across a field, they also observe the path they take to get out of the field. At the bottom of the stable field there is a stone hedge which over the years has become overgrown with couch grass. On the stable field side it is about three feet high, on the big field side because the ground is lower it is a foot higher; and I have always taken it for granted that there was no chance of the donkeys jumping over it.

This summer, however, badgers had padded down the couch grass, and made a foot-wide path up the stable field side of the hedge, then over into the big field. I half noticed its existence, even caught sight of a badger one moonlit night, as he went his way over the hedge, then on towards the sett that lies hidden in the undergrowth half-way down our cliff; but I never thought this path might give ideas to the donkeys. Geoffrey once said of them after some particular escapade: 'I knew they were educated . . . but not that educated!' And I was soon to remember his remark.

It was a pleasant July evening, and my aunt was staying with us, and we had just finished dinner; and I happened to look out of a window which is close to my desk. Far away across the moorland I saw two familiar figures on Carn Barges.

'Jeannie!' I shouted, although she was only within a few feet of me, 'the donkeys! They're on their way to Lamorna!'

There was good cause for this panicky outburst. Never before had the donkeys received such a start. If I ran it would take me the best part of ten minutes to reach them, and when they saw me coming I was certain they would take evasive action. Ingenious donkeys who had escaped from the stable field by a badger path, who were now enjoying the full flush of freedom, who knew they were on the route to the Lamorna pub, were not going to surrender tamely. And anyhow, although they had paused on Carn Barges and from a distance seemed to be meekly grazing, would they stay there long enough for me to reach them?

'They're off!'

It was Jeannie who shouted this time. She was just ahead of me as I came out of the cottage; and she caught sight of Penny leading the way down the little path from the Carn, then disappearing inland along the rough path we always went with the donkeys. We called it the donkey walk. If it had not been for the donkeys the undergrowth on either side of the winding path would have joined together, and obliterated it. But the donkeys have always liked this walk, and so I keep it open by taking a pair of secateurs along with me, snipping the tendrils of the brambles as I go. The path is like a steeplechase course. There is a point where the donkeys have to jump on to a low stone wall, then plunge into a deep gully which is always squelching with mud; and there is a stream to jump which in winter makes such a noise as it rushes downwards to the sea, that Fred at first refused to jump it. It would not stop him now, certainly not in summer when it is only a trickle.

'All I can do,' I said, 'is to take the car and meet them in Lamorna.'

'Jeannie laughed.

'You make it sound as if you are going to collect a friend who has been out for a walk.'

'I think the only thing for you to do,' I went on, 'is to walk along the path just in case they've stopped on the way.'

'All right.'

The lure of Lamorna for the donkeys lay in the potato crisps that Tommy Bailey, then landlord of the pub, provided for them; and in the carrots that Mrs Murley of the post office always offered them whenever her shop was open. They were also fussed over by numerous children, photographed by adults who rewarded them with more potato crisps, and were in fact treated as honoured guests. They loved the place. Moreover, as I will tell, they had been invited to open the annual Lamorna Gala. They felt at home in Lamorna.

But I did not find them in the village. They had lost their nerve. I had driven straight to Tommy's pub and asked those present if they had seen any donkeys, and nobody had. So I took the car up the lane which continues up the side of the valley until it fades out in moorland except for the path of the donkey walk. Halfway up I saw in the growing dusk three holidaymakers coming towards me.

'Have you,' I asked after I had stopped the car, 'by any chance seen two donkeys?'

The eccentricity of the British is their normality in unusual situations. The holidaymakers were politeness itself.

'Well,' said one in a manner that suggested I had asked whether she could tell margarine from butter, 'two donkeys did run past us earlier on.'

Ah! I said to myself, I know what has happened. They had lost their nerve on the last part of the journey to the village. Even when we were with them they had always been disconcerted. They thought a dustbin was an enemy, or the steps to a cottage, or a gutter beside the lane, or a parked car. Sometimes they would refuse to pass an object which puzzled them. They behaved, before they reached the potato crisp, like primitive tribesmen seeing the bright lights for the first time.

And so, I guessed, they had turned off on a lane to their left which ended in a cul-de-sac. I was correct. I drove the car up this lane and discovered the two of them, shame-faced, longing-to-be-home donkeys. I had no halters so I took Penny by her mane; and I frogmarched her up towards the moorland, and when I reached it Jeannie was there. We kept the donkeys ahead of us as we returned to Minack; and after they were there, after we had put them in the field above the cottage and made sure that the gate and all other possible escape routes were secure, I went back to Lamorna to collect the car.

Next morning, as had been my habit since the eggs were hatched, I peered through the barn windows to see how the young swallows were progressing. They were out of the nest.

Two were perched on top of a daffodil wind-break which was leaning against the wall opposite. The other two I could just see on the top of the galvanised bin in which we normally kept the donkey food pellets during the winter.

For three days they never flew from the barn. They used it as a nursery.

ELEVEN

When the swallows flew out of their nursery and began to play games in the sky, and perched on the slates of the stable waiting their turn for insects to be brought by their parents, the shine on the green of the bracken was fading, docks were seeding, the bulb meadows needed scything, the cuckoos were soon to leave, the brightness of butterflies had taken the place of June gaiety of birds. Early July time, and the mood of Cornwall was changing. Cars rushed along the narrow lanes, meeting at places too narrow to pass where drivers shouted at each other, each refusing to be the first to back. It is always the same in the first half of July. The visitors are in a hurry. They seem to have brought their grievances with them.

'Why the hell do you have this stone post here?' demanded a driver of a friend of mine. He had just smashed into it.

'It's my gatepost,' replied my friend plaintively. She produced a hammer to help beat out the damaged mudguard, found a glass of milk for the child in the car, carried a cup of tea to the mother.

'Ugh,' said the mother after sipping it, 'you've put sugar into it. I don't take sugar.'

'The gatepost should never have been there in this narrow lane,' went on the husband, bringing the hammer down with a bang, and breaking it. 'And why have a cheap hammer?'

At night the entrances to fields, the laybys, the grass verges, are the parking places of caravans disguised as cars. In the morning they disgorge their occupants who eat out of tins brought from home, then leave their litter for County Council workmen laboriously to collect. During the day other cars are parked; and men in braces, women in flowered dresses, enjoy their Cornish holiday by the roadside, brewing tea on Calor gas camp stoves, sitting on the metal-framed chairs that fold neatly in the boot of the car, reading newspapers.

Early July time . . . and one local inhabitant will say to another: 'A lot of people about but they aren't spending any money.'

A publican will interrupt.

'Three nice looking people came into the pub yesterday lunchtime, said they were thirsty but didn't ask for beer. They asked for three glasses of water, and although I didn't like this I didn't want to be awkward and so I obliged them. They carried the glasses outside and sat on the bench. Then I saw them through the window dropping those lemon powders or some other flavour into the glasses. They didn't even bother to bring the glasses back when they left.'

A café proprietor betters the story.

'A couple asked for a cup of tea. Then shared it.' And he added, 'Never mind, a better lot will start coming next week.'

The local inhabitants can be edgy in early July time, thinking of overdrafts to be cleared by the season's end;

110

and, unused to city manners, they are sometimes inclined to take offence when offence was not intended. Sometimes, of course, they are also accused of being greedy, but the friendliest people in the world towards strangers who want to be friendly too; but they are quick to react against those whose manners they consider abrupt or supercilious. But the pleasant stranger will always be made to feel welcome; and he will find certain aspects of the Cornish character, politeness and enthusiasm for instance, that will charm him.

Cornwall, however, is puzzled about its future. Should it be a playground, a haven for retired people, and an agricultural county, or should it become industrialised? Areas of Cornwall are, of course, already industrialised . . . china clay around St Austell, engineering in Camborne, the ship repairing docks at Falmouth, the developing tin industry; and there are factories for light industries, often subsidised by the Government, on the outskirts of many other towns. But there are those who would like to see such industrialisation substantially increased pointing out that this is the only way that the young of Cornwall will be able to find work in the county. There are others who argue that the native young, like their forebears, consider it adventurous to leave home; and that although some will want to stay, there will be a negligible number to staff the new industries. Hence labour will have to be imported with all its attendant social problems; and values, which hitherto have provided the Cornish with happiness, will be destroyed.

Propagandists for more industrialisation also make capital out of the unemployment figures which are above the national average. These figures were increased by SET, and by higher basic national wage rates; for no local employer can now afford to keep a person on his staff who does not give his maximum effort in return. Nevertheless the figures give a misleading impression of the true situation. Cornwall is so pleasant a place to live in that there are unemployed who are quite content to remain unemployed. There are also the seasonal unemployed. Fishermen who sign on as unemployed when the weather is unsuitable for their vessels to go to sea, those who work in the holiday trade during the summer, then take a holiday themselves during the winter.

111

All these inflate the unemployment figures. Few of them, I fancy, would exchange their present way of living for a life in a factory. For better or for worse they believe, deep within themselves, that they have a sounder philosophy than those who live in industrial centres; and when every summer the roar of the holidaymaker comes to Cornwall, the wisdom of this belief seems to be confirmed. Holidaymakers do not suggest that those who earn high wages in monotonous conditions are to be envied. A sophisticated society, it appears, has to lose its soul as a price for the transient rewards it worships.

The policy makers of Cornwall, meanwhile, are pressing for a trunk road (a spine road they call it) through Cornwall to Penzance. The prospect of a bonanza of motor cars being able to speed to this end of Britain excites them. Faith in communications, in the form of motorways and trunk roads, is the vogue; and a trunk road to Penzance therefore suits the age. But those of us who live in West Cornwall wonder what is to happen to the traffic when it reaches Penzance. For ten months in the year there is not enough traffic to cause any trouble, but in high summer the town is already a bottleneck. There is a talk of a by-pass round the town, and that poses another problem. What happens to the traffic when it reaches the few narrow roads and lanes on the other side of the town in the wild, rural district of West Penwith? But perhaps the prospective chaos does not matter. Perhaps the object of spending vast sums on a trunk road is to make industrialisation inevitable. Factories, and new housing estates, will have to line the route to justify the expense. Materialism accompanied by its vandalism, will be victorious.

Sometimes I lightheartedly wonder whether the small though influential pressure for industrialisation stems from the stark religious convictions of the Cornish past, when pleasure was considered a sin. All those grim services in draughty chapels, all those heady revivalist meetings where sinners suddenly saw the light, perhaps still echo down the years. Everywhere there are reminders of those days. Small chapels isolated in the corners of fields, great barn-like chapels in main streets, even posters on noticeboards still exhort the passersby to behave according to the scriptures. 'Steer clear of alcohol and you will steer clear of trouble.' 'Keep to the narrow path and you will do no wrong.' And there are too, along with this haunting religious fervour, reminders of the industrial times that belonged to it. Desolate mine stacks are scattered around West Cornwall, prodding into the sky like headstones in a cemetery, a constant reminder to every Cornishman that in the nineteenth century the Cornish mining and engineering traditions were known throughout the world.

Perhaps this is the reason why local dignitaries, from time to time, refer to the holiday trade in terms that suggest they are almost ashamed of it, as if it were a trade of immoral earnings. You can also hear disparaging remarks about the ageing population of retired people with which Cornwall is allegedly burdened. This is a viewpoint I can never understand. People are going to retire somewhere after working hard all their lives, and Cornwall is lucky to attract so many. They bring their savings with them and, most importantly, they spend their income in the county. Retired people, a holiday industry . . . this impression of a lotus land is offensive to some. Yet the holiday industry is already worth £42 million a year, and future expansion could be enormous, particularly if it set out to attract people from abroad. It needs, however, just as much practical encouragement from the Government of the day as the Government now gives to build factories.

Meanwhile the Cornwall County Council is giving a lead. It is trying to centralise all aspects of the holiday trade under its advisory control; and in taking this action it is following the example of such holiday areas as Bermuda and the Bahamas. Both are geographically part of the West Indies, just as Cornwall is geographically part of the South West; but such are their individual attractions they prefer to operate each on their own. Cornwall, too, with its special attractions, must act on its own.

The County Council, therefore, will supply the driving force behind such essentials of the holiday business as publicity, tours by travel agents from abroad, and other aspects of business promotion that can best be developed by a centralised Cornish organisation. It is also compiling a register of high standard accommodation in hotels, guest houses and farms throughout Cornwall and the Scilly Islands for distribution among potential holidaymakers at home and abroad. Support will have to be given to the Council if it is to carry out its programme, and here is the rub. Until the success of the Council's plans are proven, those in the holiday industry are loth to subscribe towards the expense; and if they dither and do nothing, the enthusiasm of the County Council may wane; and instead of the holiday playground it aims to create, the earth moving machines will proceed to eat up the rich agricultural lands, destroying the countryside and the magic of Cornwall. Then the holiday industry will fade away, and the inhabitants will remember with nostalgia their present spirit of independence as they trudge towards the factory gates. Those in the holiday trade may be edgy in early July time, but such edginess does not last long. Soon the visitors begin to arrive who are free spending, and business begins to boom, and Cornwall is giving pleasure to tens of thousands of people. Surely such an industry imaginatively developed is worth far more to the Cornish both financially and spiritually, then a multitude of factories.

Jeannie and I, meanwhile, remain in our private world. We discuss solemn problems, argue about them with others, but are happiest when we pretend they do not exist. It is easy to pretend when we are up on the bridge. Each day, each hour, each minute the scene is different in the kingdom around us. This is the glory of living in the present, of having the time to marvel at the grace of a buzzard, at the sight of a Peacock butterfly, first of the summer, settling for a second on a leaf of the escallonia beside us, at the shape of a cloud above the Lizard; and relishing sudden excitements like watching the perambulations of Whitepants, the fox who lived on the other side of the shallow valley in the copse where the magpies had their cumbersome nest.

He was a fine dog fox with a splendid red-brown coat and brush. He looked, in fact, quite a normal fox until you saw his haunches, and these were a light fawn colour like a tropical khaki. He was a comical sight, half noble, half a

114

clown; and he had an unusual temperament for a fox. He was clearly an easy going, placid character who had faith in the good nature of everyone in the neighbourhood; and as a result he courted danger unnecessarily. He was also a punctual fox. He used to appear, this July, from his hideout in the copse at six every evening on the dot; and so when I saw him I did not have to look at my watch to know it was news time. Whitepants and the time signal coincided.

He would then proceed to potter in the field beside the copse, a field in which potatoes had been grown until a month before and where the dried up tops of potato plants still strewed the ground, and where the jackdaws and the crows pecked at the potatoes that had been left behind after the harvesting. Jeannie and I would sit on the bridge, evening drinks beside us, with our field-glasses trained on him, watching his every move and observing his intelligent face. Occasionally he would turn his attention to the hedge, and like a cat he would poise himself to pounce on some mysterious rustle, and after a tantalising minute of waiting he would leap forward. There he would be, spreadeagled, motionless. 'He's missed it,' one of us would say.

He would move on through the gap to the big field of green grass opposite us, and there the young rabbits of summer would see him coming; and they would stop nibbling, and those who were close would scurry away, and others would sit upright like begging dogs, half afraid, half curious. Sometimes he would make a dart at one of them, a half-hearted rush which suggested he had made the move because it was expected of him, not because he wanted a rabbit for his supper. Indeed this was what puzzled us about Whitepants. Why set off on a journey when there were still hours of daylight to provide danger?

It was, too, the time of day when a young man or two would be out with their guns; and from over the brow of the hill we would hear a shot, and we would glance at an unperturbed Whitepants nosing in the grass, and we were the ones who were afraid. Then a few minutes later we would see a young man silhouetted against the skyline, advancing towards the field, and we were aware that he would be able to hide on the other side of the hedge at the top; and both

Whitepants and the rabbits would be in view. You cannot blame a farmer for shooting a fox when his chickens have been repeatedly raided. You can understand him being furious with someone like myself who scares the fox away just as the shot is about to be fired; and thus scares the rabbits away too.

However, after a while, after becoming so accustomed to Whitepants that I felt it my duty to protect an interfering nuisance, I could not stand the tension any longer; and when, one evening, I saw the young man advancing again, I left the bridge, ran down the lane, and up the slope to the field towards him. I was trespassing. I had no right to be there. Nor, as it turned out, had I any need to be there.

I was out of breath when I reached him.

'Please,' I managed to gasp. 'Please don't shoot the fox you see down here very evening . . . it's a fox we know very well and we're very fond of him.'

I felt foolish. I realised I sounded a little hysterical; and that it would have been so much more dignified had I walked slowly, nonchalantly up the field, and conveyed my feelings after a few casual words of introduction.

'I won't harm him,' said the young man, and he looked at me good humouredly, the same sort of way that an indulgent father might look at an over eager son, 'I don't shoot foxes anyway.'

Whitepants had a neighbour in his copse, a dog fox who lolloped around on three legs; the fourth, although not completely useless, barely touched the ground when he was moving. We did not see him often, and we certainly never saw him in the company of Whitepants; but from time to time we noticed him edging along the shelter of the hedge, then into the copse and out of sight. He may, of course, have been on passage to the cliff and the route through the copse was a convenient one to take. He may, on the other hand, have been a relation that Whitepants did not like, or a visitor that had outstayed his welcome, or just an old fox whose time was up. All I can say is that one late afternoon, about half an hour before Whitepants was due to make his customary appearance, a hyena-like sound came shrieking from the copse, accompanied by fox barks, and a general

116

thunderous noise of battle. Once before I had heard such a din. We were bunching daffodils late one night when there was a terrible cacophony up the lane; and it went on so long that finally I went with a torch to have a look. Half way up the light shone on a fox in the ditch. It was dying. An old fox killed by a young one.

On this occasion I took no steps to investigate. I had a good view from where I was standing on the bridge, and so I just stared at the copse, and waited. The noise stopped just as suddenly as it started. Then a second or two later I caught sight of the three-legged fox emerging from the copse into the field, and he was slinking along as if he were ashamed of something which had just happened. Then I saw him stop, and sit down and lick himself . . . onwards a few yards and the same anxious licking. Otherwise, although I was looking at him through my field-glasses, I could see no sign of any wound on him. He reached a broken down part of the hedge, and hopped through it into the green carpet of bracken, and disappeared from my sight. I never saw him again.

Half an hour later, punctually at six o'clock, Whitepants appeared. A suave, unperturbed Whitepants. No detective observing his serene manner, would have guessed he had so recently been guilty of violent assault. Or had he been guilty? My thoughts may have been maligning him all the while. Perhaps he had been sound asleep in his earth. Perhaps he was just waking up when he heard this noise up above. A third fox, face to face with my three-legged fox on the track through the copse to the cliff, may have been the attacker. I will never know. This is the maddening, delicious part of living in the country close to nature . . . there are so many unanswered questions. One does not have the mind of a scientist, ponderously seeking logical explanations, or coldly coming to confident conclusions which in a few years are proved to be wrong.

I do not know, for instance, what happened to Whitepants. Throughout that summer he continued to follow his routine, and it was a routine as I have said that had its dangers. A fox, if he is wise, does not wander out on a summer's evening, then follow a route which takes him straight past farms where milking is just finishing, where tired, even irritable, farmers are about to have their supper. It is something a sensible fox, a fox always alert to fear, simply would not do. Whitepants acted otherwise.

After he had made his gestures at pursuing the rabbits, after he had no doubt watched me making my out of breath pleas for his safety, he continued his dangerous way. He quietly, ruminatively, sniffed around the field, then jumped the hedge into a no man's land of gorse and brambles, and became hidden from my sight. Not quite. The magpies followed him when he hopped that hedge, after I had been watching him, the magpies took over the watch. I stood on the bridge listening to them chattering as they displayed his secret whereabouts from above. Every evening the same disclosures were made. Were others aware of them as well?'

A fox has a fascination for a magpie. I have seen so often a magpie hopping about in a field where a fox is roaming, baiting the fox, cackling insults at it. A pair of magpies had always made a special point of baiting Whitepants who continued his perambulations without taking notice. Indeed a family of magpies used to dance around him. No doubt they came from the cumbersome nest above his earth; and I wonder what they thought when one day, later in the summer, he did not appear. I know that Jeannie and I missed him as we sat on the bridge. Poor Whitepants. He should never have begun his nocturnal adventures in daylight.

TWELVE

We seldom leave Minack during the summer even for a day. Once a week Jeannie shops to fill the larder; and as we have a refrigerator with a small deep freeze compartment, such weekly shopping presents no problem. Nor do we have to worry about fresh bread because Jeannie bakes it herself, or milk which we have from Jack's farm at the top of the lane (from the milk Jeannie makes her own Cornish cream), or about vegetables because we grow our own. Nor do we have to queue at the laundry. We have an automatic washing machine which merrily does its work while Jeannie performs some task of her own; and the contents are then hung on the washing line, up above the well, and when they are dry they have the salty scent of sea air.

There is still, however, shopping to do; and every Friday morning Jeannie drives up the lane on her way to call at Ted Chappel's in St Buryan, or Jackson's in Sennen, or Jim Veal in Newlyn where she buys fish landed that morning, or Reg Stevens the butcher whose shop faces the river beside Newlyn Bridge. All these have the pleasant atmosphere associated with small shops, where as you make your choice, national events of the past week are discussed and local gossip exchanged. No one is in a hurry. Care is taken that you have exactly what you require. The mood is conveyed that shopping is to be enjoyed and not to be anxious about. You leave looking forward to your return, despite the fact that prices next week will have risen again.

In Penzance Jeannie parks the car in the car park behind the Greenmarket. Penzance is still a charming old market town although one wonders how long it can maintain its character. A monstrous skyscraper, housing government departments, now looms above the rooftops in the centre of the town. The route of a new road round the harbour will, if the plan is implemented, demolish many old houses including perhaps the one in Chapel Street from which Maria Branwell set off for Yorkshire to meet and Marry Patrick Brontë. The entry into Penzance along Eastern Green is already a conglomeration of utility factory buildings, a garish petrol station, and a caravan site that looks like a shanty town. More significantly, long established shops are one by one closing down unable to compete with SET and the invasion of supermarket chain stores; and thus old buildings disappear and Market Jew Street, the main street of Penzance, is becoming like any suburban High Street. But what value has antiquity in this age of landings on the moon.

The latest plan to hasten on the changing face of Penzance is a diabolical one . . . the Central Electricity Generating Board propose to transport huge transformers through the town from the harbour on giant trailers destined for various booster power stations in Cornwall. The Board has intimated that on sections of the route where it is too narrow for the trailers, the offendings buildings will be compulsorily purchased; and pulled down. The fact that the buildings contain shops, that people will lose their livelihood does not seem to matter. For the moment the buildings have been reprieved, but one wonders for how long. Whatever happens, the fact that the proposal was made is an example of what planners are prepared to do in the name of progress.

There is still, however, the friendliness of Penzance to be grateful for, the pleasure of watching people strolling instead of hurrying; and there are the sudden moments of beauty when you catch sight of the sea through the slit of a street, one of the narrow streets falling downhill towards the harbour and Mount's Bay; or you may be stirred by a glimpse of St Michael's Mount away in the distance by Marazion; or you may see the Scillonian, white and elegant like a tiny cruising liner, setting off for the islands; or you may notice a ship anchored in the Bay which is a stranger, and you are momentarily puzzled as to why she is there. The emotions are stirred too by the small Regency houses that you find in odd corners of the town, and by the Morrab Gardens where near-tropical plants blossom, even by the promenade which stretches from the harbour to Newlyn, rebuilt after the great storm of 1962, and now the finest in the west country. There is still much to delight in Penzance.

Jeannie's weekly visit, however, does not last long, and this not because she does not enjoy it. It is simply that shops she used to go to have disappeared; and now her regular visits are limited to friends like Mrs Michell who keeps the newspaper shop up the steps from the terrace of Market Jew Street, and the staff at Peasgoods, Neil James of Davy's, and the girls at Leroy; and there are occasional visits to see Mr Simpson about buying a shirt for me, and to Mr Nicholls the ironmonger, to Mr Dunne of the photography shop, to Gerry of the Post Office at the bottom of the town, to Mr Cousins in Alexandra Road, and to the remarkable Michells the jewellers who seem to repair any watch, any small piece of jewellery for kindness instead of for profit; and on the way home she may look in at the Queens Hotel on the front where she used to go as a child before sailing to the Scillies; and where Frank the barman and Billy the porter are still there to fuss over her. The Queens is our headquarters in Penzance. Jeannie always goes there, as I do, whenever she has to make a long distance telephone call.

She will also have seen Charlie Brockway during her visit. Charlie Brockway is a black and white cat of substantial stature, a notorious personality in the town, whom you meet sometimes striding along the terrace in Market Jew Street, or lurking in Morrab Gardens, or sauntering along the West Parade between Alexandra Road and the car park behind the Greenmarket.

It is in the car park, however, where you will generally find him. This is his patch. This is where he will stretch himself on the bonnet of a car and refuse to move when the owner is wishing to leave. He has a particular fondness for vans, large vans; and it is fortunate for him that only local vans use the car park, and the drivers, knowing his eccentricities, look out for him, both inside and outside their vans, before they move off. Even so I have seen a van move off with Charlie curled on the bonnet, and the driver laughing, and tooting his horn, ready to stop as soon as Charlie woke up.

His home is the shoe shop from which he takes his name. The front faces Chapel Street, the back the car park; and the wall which separates the back from the car park is where Charlie holds court, where he washes in leisurely confidence, pretending to be indifferent to the noises of praise from his admirers, who pause by him, hoping for recognition, shopping bags in hand. There are many like Jeannie who look forward to seeing Charlie Brockway, and when he is not there on the wall or on the bonnet of a car, the car park attendant will be questioned: 'Where's Charlie?' The attendant, himself an admirer, will reply inconsequentially: 'Yesterday that Charlie caused some trouble . . . ' and he will tell another of Charlie's adventures.

He was a stray before he came into his world of shoes. He was looking through the door of the shop one day when a lady assistant showed an interest in him. This alerted his instinct of self-preservation; and he proceeded to behave in that irresistible, beguiling fashion that strays adopt once they have decided on the home that suits them. The shoe shop would be his home, he decided, and nothing would stop him. Of course, the assistants were only too happy to oblige, and so too were the customers. They were delighted that such a beautiful cat should take such an interest in their stockinged feet; and so Charlie wandered at will during the day, but was sure to be home by closing time. He had a job to do. He was night custodian of the shoes; and he clearly enjoyed this role. But on one occasion he was faced with a situation that all night watchmen hope will never occur. A thief broke into the shop. Nothing serious was stolen. Perhaps the sight of Charlie advancing towards him, claws at the ready, frightened the man off. Whatever may have happened, the reaction of both staff and customers next morning when the theft was discovered was the same. 'What about Charlie?' was the cry instead of 'What has been stolen?' . . . 'Was Charlie frightened? Poor Charlie!' There has been a touch of glamour about Charlie ever since.

One day before the end of July we went to the Scillies to see Jane. A day away from Minack always requires serious preparation, for it upsets the peaceful routine. Thus it was arranged that Geoffrey would do work close to the cottage, would stay on after his normal time, then lock the gate near Monty's Leap when he left. He would keep a close eye on Boris, feed him with his favourite digestive biscuits, and shut him inside his house at the end of the day. The donkeys, meanwhile, would be kept in the stable field because they would be sure to hoot if any strangers came up towards the cottage from the big field; and thus Geoffrey would be alerted if he had not seen the strangers himself. Lama, of course, would be well fed before we set out, but a window would be kept open for her; and Geoffrey would try and keep track of her peregrinations during the day, and would make sure that she was inside the cottage, and the window shut, when he departed. The gulls were provided for by a plate of Jeannie's home-made bread, so Geoffrey would toss them a piece whenever their squawks became too prolonged; and the small birds of the bird table had a Michael Truscott designed pottery dish full of grain from which Geoffrey could feed them. All this organisation because of a day away from the premises. An example of what happens when your life becomes so pleasantly parochial that you deem such matters of high importance.

The purpose of the visit was to attend the christening of Jane's daughter Sylvia. We were godparents and it is understandable that we were pleased. Jane had been part of a turbulent period of our life at Minack. I remember her arriving with her mother, a fey woman of indomitable courage to live in the middle cottage of the three at Pentewan, her mother having taken up the job of herdswoman at the farm; and they brought with them a caravanserai of animals. Lamb, the sheep who was given a hut in the garden, Siamese Sim, and Val the white Persian, Eva the griffon, half blind and personal dog to Jane, a parrot who once belonged to Jane's great-grandmother, and Acid, a brindle bull terrier, who was to play for hours every day in the fields above the sea with Jane's young brother Jeremy.

Jane was at boarding school at the time, but within a few months she would be fifteen, and when she learnt about our flower farm, she decided she would like to work for us; although her headmistress had high ambitions for her future, pressing her to stay on at school, Jane was adamant; and after she had won her mother over to her view, she arrived one day at Minack. We did not need her help, we could not even afford her. But there she was and she became a part of our lives . . . and I can see her now with fair hair falling over her shoulders arriving across the fields from her cottage with a puzzled Boris in her arms after an admirer had brought him for her dinner; and coming up from the cliff in a storm of rain, basket of daffodils in either hand, her face hidden by a black sou'wester much too big for her; and sharing the excitement with Jeannie as they prepared the flowers for the Penzance Show (the prize cards we won line the oak beam above me as I write); and then her moment of triumph after she had left us and gone to Tresco Gardens, when she won the Prince of Wales' Cup at the Show, the most important cup for any grower to win, and she was the youngest ever to do so. Understandable, therefore, that there was a special pleasure in this visit to the Scillies.

She lived now on the island of Bryher, her mother had

died, Dick, her husband, worked on one of the small flower farms, and in his spare time was a craftsman in woodwork. He met us in St Mary's after we had flown from Penzance in the helicopter, and he had a launch ready to take us to Bryher. I had never been to any of the outer islands before, and as the launch splashed through the sun-sparkled water, I suppose it was inevitable that I should begin thinking of my time in the South Seas. Small yachts, some flying foreign flags, lay anchored around us as we passed, reminding me of those I watched from my hotel window in Papeete, conveying the impression of adventure, snugness, hot days, danger, all in one. There was the island of St Martins to my right in the distance, heaving out of the sea like Bora Bora, and everywhere were the small, uninhabited rocks of islands which were like the coral reefs of the Tuomotus. Samson was to my left with its white beach like Toopua, and opposite Bryher was the green land of Tresco, lush like the hinterland of Tahiti. And when the launch hove-to off the long beach of Bryher, and we jumped into a rowing boat to be rowed ashore, and the keel of the rowing boat crunched against the sand, this primitive arrival took the years away from me; and my senses, if not my eyes, at that moment belonged to other arrivals, other islands.

Jeannie used to come to Bryher when she was a young girl. Her father, although he never stayed there, had a passion for it; and when he built a house in St Albans at the top of the hill in Avenue Road, he called it Bryher Lodge; and if that was not enough to prove his affection for the island, he called a week-end cottage at East Mersea, Bryher Cottage. The family used to holiday at the Atlantic Hotel on St Mary's, then make frequent picnic expeditions to Bryher; and on one of them they bought a set of exquisite lace mats, crocheted by a very old lady called Aunt Sarah. Aunt Sarah caught Jeannie's imagination, partly because her hands were crippled with arthritis and Jeannie marvelled how she did her delicate work, partly because she had lived all her life on the island. A Hans Andersen character, Jeannie thought, and she used to talk to me about her until I was tired of the telling. We have the mats now at Minack. And we walked by the cottage where she used to live, on the way to Jane on the other side of the island.

'Jane!' called Dick as he opened the door of their home, 'Jane!'

The christening, of course, was an important event in the island, and so it was the hostess Jane who greeted us, not the Jane who preferred to walk about barefooted on hot summer days, who cared nothing for the urban ways of living. For a day such moods were forgotten, and it was an absurdly young looking Jane in a cyclamen pink dress who showed us the baby in the cot; and then went on preparing the delicacies for those who were coming back after the service. Jeannie, in due course, said the cake might have been produced by Fortnums; and Jane then explained that she had taken the precaution of first making another one, a trial run over the target; and it had been a disaster. There were delicious canapes and sandwiches and wine; and all the more pleasant to enjoy because of the knowledge that the feast had to be planned far ahead. In Bryher you cannot say you will have a party, then go into the High Street to buy what you want.

But these pleasures came after the service in the church built in the eighteenth century, close to the beach, the oldest church in use in the Scillies, to which we walked, Sylvia in a carry-cot between her parents. I am no church-goer although the ambience of churches, of whatever denomination, have a deep significance for me. Here among the stone arches, altars, painted glass windows, ancient fonts, and musty smells, the mood of timelessness reaches into your secret depths; but for me this is not achieved when I worship in the mass. I find myself instead looking forward to the end of a hymn, or a sermon, or the service itself. My mind wanders, I am a spectator and not a participant. Perhaps this is because religion was made into a weapon of punishment when I was a schoolboy at Harrow; and instead of the Bible being an adventure to read, for instance, it became a menace. Copying out verses of the Bible, several times over, was frequently the fate of those boys who had erred; and the memory of this tedious task has remained with me for ever. Nor were the services any more enjoyable. They were a bore, in fact, until the last verse of the last hymn

126

when we knew there were only minutes left before we were released.

I prefer, therefore, to be alone in a church instead of being one of a congregation, although there are other times, at services for special occasions, when I am easily emotionally involved. For me, indeed, there must be a reason for churchgoing; and that reason will involve an individual . . . a wedding, a funeral, or a christening. But the conventional service has little meaning for me. I feel closer to God when I am in some beautiful corner of Minack without anyone in sight.

We walked back to the cottage after the service. Friends strung out along the path, the sea in sight, the parson whose first christening on Bryher it had been, strolling along with us . . . living on Tresco he had come by boat for the occasion. There are of course no cars on Bryher, and when Jane was married she travelled in her bridal dress to the church on a tractor. Thus we wandered along, a happy, unselfconscious procession; and I am glad we have a memento of the day.

I had admired the many examples of Dick's craftsmanship in the cottage, beautiful woodwork which communicated the patience and skill of those who worked wood long ago; and when I happened to say that I admired one piece of craftsmanship, I did not expect he had noted what I said. 'You must sell these beautiful things,' I had urged, 'the tourists would love them surely.' His reply was non-committal. Or perhaps he was being modest. Or he felt the tourists wouldn't pay the price to cover the time, labour, and material expense of the work. Whatever went through his mind, he did however realise that we admired his talent; and so he thought he would like to give us some pleasure. The following Christmas a small oak jewellery box arrived at Minack, lined with red baize, and inscribed: 'Made from materials from s. s. *Mando* wrecked Golden Ball, Scilly, 1955.'

THIRTEEN

High summer, and the end is beginning. The elder flowers
have turned into berries, the apples are fattening, the tomato
plants have only the top trusses to ripen, the air sing with
insect sounds, flies bother the donkeys, convolvulus is
winding up the camellia bush beside the rose garden, up
the fuchsia and the honeysuckle in front of the cottage,
up any plant or bush it can find; bees fill themselves with
honey from the mignonette on the bridge, multi-coloured
nasturtiums tumble over rocks, night-scented stock and
tobacco plants romanticise the evenings. There still seems
much of summer ahead . . . but the swifts are gathering,
briefest of our bird visitors, and any evening they will be
spiralling into the sky above Minack, calling their shrill cry

of farewell, higher and higher, until they disappear in the fading light.

I no longer hear the cuckoo. I was walking with Jeannie and the donkeys along the path towards Lamorna when I saw the last cuckoo of summer, three of them in fact; a before-breakfast walk, and the fishing boats were passing below us, hastening to Newlyn fish market. I saw them perched on the rocks of Carn Barges and for a moment I thought they were woodpigeons. Then I realised my mistake and I called softly to Jeannie and we stopped; and as I did so Fred nudged me in the back, so I put a hand over his muzzle which he knows to be a signal for quiet. We stood there and watched, then away the cuckoos went, flying south. 'Jeannie!' I had called, in a fit of sadness as they took off, 'hold on to their tails!' And we both laughed at my nonsense.

The swallows remained. Our brood still flew gaily together around Minack, playing their games in the sky, chasing each other high above the stable field and away over the green tops of the elm trees, out of sight, and back again, swerving, dipping, twisting; and suddenly they would be tired and they would swoop down on the electricity cable connecting the cottage, and settle side by side twittering for a minute or two; then off again. At night they still roosted in the barn, clustering together on a beam, but they were not to be there for much longer. Their parents shooed them off. The eggs of the second brood had been laid in the same nest, three of them; and when they were hatched, the barn was a nursery again.

There was another nest, a greenfinch nest, in the fork of the elm above Boris's pond. Jeannie, for some reason, has a special fondness for greenfinches. She loves their plaintive call, but although we hear this call off and on throughout the summer, they never seem to nest with us until late in the season. Once, in an August, a pair of greenfinches had a nest in the same fork of the same tree above Boris's pond. It was a cold, wet August, and I remember that when the brood of four were about ready to fly a vicious easterly gale blew up. It was so fierce that it was a marvel that the nest was not blown away, and the brood with it; but during the second day of the gale, orders were given to abandon ship. The nest that evening was empty.

The following morning was sunny and still and we heard the plaintive greenfinch cries in the wood, and thought all was well; but as Jeannie was walking to the small greenhouse to weigh tomatoes, she saw a movement in the grass, and there near the foot of the elm was a baby greenfinch. It was sick. Its eyes were half closed, and its head nodded, and it had all the signs of a bird that had not long to live. Jeannie picked it up and placed it in a box full of hay in the greenhouse, then managed to put a few drops of Exultation of Flowers down its throat by gently holding its beak open with her fingers. The vet happened to call that morning, and so she asked his advice; and he told her that her treatment was correct, except that he had never heard of Exultation of Flowers (it is a secret blending of flower juices and it comes from Nairn in Scotland); and he added that as the sun was now shining, it would be a good idea to leave the invalid and its box outside the greenhouse during the day so that the parents would be able to feed it naturally.

This we did. There was no risk of Lama attacking it although the box was on the ground. Lama, never in her life, has shown any greed for catching birds; like Monty before her. Boris would have been more of a danger; but Boris at the time was having a love affair with a patch of ground near his hut which meant he would not be waddling towards the small greenhouse. Boris was like that. A patch of ground was sacrosanct for a while, then on to another.

So during the day the parents fussed over the invalid, and at night we carried it into the greenhouse out of the evening damp air. Then one afternoon we saw the invalid hop out of the box, and we had to retrieve it. The next day it flew up on to the low wall close to Boris's pool; and we retrieved it again. Another day and we couldn't find it anywhere.

This story might have been forgotten by us but for the outcome three weeks later. Jeannie was sitting on the white seat beside the verbena bush when she heard a surge of plaintive cries coming from the elder tree which is next to the verbena. She looked up and saw six greenfinches within

130

a few feet of her. Two grown up, and four young all in a row, facing her. Jeannie has a fanciful mind, but I believe her assertion that they were singing her a song of thank you.

There was no such incident this summer. No gale to disturb the nest. No sign of any touble among the fledgelings. We kept watch, of course, and we would point out the nest to visitors, and the children among the visitors would listen gravely as we told the story of the young greenfinch of another year. And then I would tell them other stories like that of one-eyed Billy the robin who, after being in the neighbourhood for a couple of years and a regular at the bird table, had a fight with another robin; and received the worst of it. He found his way to the door of the cottage, and I nearly stepped on him as I came out of the cottage, a crumpled handful of feathers. He too was taken to the small greenhouse; and we kept him in an óld chicken coop with a wire front until we thought he was well enough to live on his own again. Unfortunately we were too hasty. No sooner was one-eyed Billy set free than his enemy pounced on him again; and had I not been there to see the attack, Billy certainly would have been killed. His enemy was vicious, pinning him to the ground, and pecking furiously at him. So I rescued him again, and this time he was in the coop until he was as strong as any rival except for his one eye; and when I took him to the greenhouse door and let him go, he flew off merrily into the wood. We saw him from time to time for several months afterwards; but there came a very cold spring, and we never saw him again.

We had a nest of hedgehogs also this summer. I had never seen a hedgehog in the neighbourhood before, and I had no knowledge of their habits; and when one night I heard squeaks from under the floorboards of our spare room, I called out to Jeannie in alarm: 'Rats! We've got rats!'

Our spare room is unusual. It was designed as a chicken house, but it is now connected with the cottage at one end, and with the bathroom at the other. When we bought it we were advised to erect it on some kind of base so that the floor was off the ground, thus keeping it safe from damp. We, therefore, collected a number of large stones or small rocks, built six blocks from them, three for each side, then levelled the floor of the chicken house upon them. There has always been, therefore, a gap between floor and earth; and it was from within this gap that there came the squeaks.

In such a situation one hopes the problem will solve itself. The rats, I prayed, were only temporary visitors, and they would soon run off elsewhere; but the noise persisted and I began to be worried. On the second night the squeaks were louder than ever though without doubt they seemed to be happy squeaks, game playing squeaks, and Jeannie and I wondered whether our rat theory might possibly be wrong. But what other animal *would* make such a noise in such a place? It was obvious that I would have to investigate in the morning.

In the morning we were woken up by a piercing scream. It sounded like a child reacting to a moment of terror. Silence for a second, then the scream again. We hastened outside, half thinking it might be the scream of a rabbit caught by a stoat; but such a scream does not last long, the rabbit dies too quickly. Scream! There it was again.

The donkeys who had spent the night in the field beside the cottage were now as interested in the scream as we were; and when I saw Fred, ears alert, staring intently at a spot outside the bathroom I hurried towards him. 'What's up, Fred?' I asked, 'have you found out?'

He had. Outside the bathroom was a drain, and this drain was hidden from sight by a wooden cover. Scream! The sound came from under the cover. I bent down and lifted it up. To my astonishment, trapped in the drain's basin was a baby hedgehog.

So we no longer had to worry about the squeaks from under the spare room; and at night we would go out with a torch and catch sight of the hedgehog family drinking the milk from the saucer placed there by Jeannie. They were nervous creatures. They scampered back to their nest within a second of the torch lighting upon them. Then later, as I sat in my bath, I would hear their squeaks again as they played.

Every day, now that the holiday season was at its height, we were greeting strangers. This aspect of our life now played so dominant a part in the daily curriculum that we could make no plans without considering it. We would expect to be on our own up to eleven o'clock in the morning, but after that hour we were likely to have callers any time to dusk. There was no question of taking a couple of hours off together and going down to the sea for a bathe, or having a picnic on the rocks; for Geoffrey would soon be shouting from the top of the cliff that someone was waiting to see us. Nor could we pursue any particular task for long. Once upon a time we would have been helping Geoffrey dig the bulbs at this period of the year or taking part in some other acitivity on the land, but this was impossible when interruptions were regular throughout the day. We had to be on duty. We were always half listening for a car coming down the lane, or half watching for a figure coming up to the cottage door. Yet if we had not remained always available, those who had come considerable distances would have found the place empty; and we had had enough experience to know that this could cause disappointment.

The question is, however, why bother in any case? It was far too demanding a routine for the reason to be that of vanity. Naturally we were pleased that people should want to meet us, should make the effort to plan their holidays so that they could come and discuss subjects they believed provided a common interest; but it was not the kind of fleeting flattery that a film star receives when asked for his autograph. We were involved with these people who came; and so we had an acute sense of our own inadequacy. If someone had come a long way, had to search for our whereabouts, who knew all about us though we knew nothing about them, who was prepared to accept a rebuff after walking down the long lane in the event of us not reacting in the way it was hoped . . . it was natural we should feel inadequate. Years ago I had discovered that life is sad rather than funny; and that, when a stranger wants to meet you, one should always remember this. Hence, when a stranger came advancing towards me, rather shyly and apologising for the intrusion, I was aware of other occasions in other years when I myself wanted a welcome.

The gain, however, is mutual. Jeannie and I have met a

133

far larger cross-section of people than ever would have been the case had we lived in a city; and as a consequence we have had the opportunity to listen to views and experiences that otherwise would have been denied us. In a week taken at random during the summer, there were among the strangers who came down the lane: a computer designer, a young prison warder, a matron of a hospital, a parson, three schoolmasters, the head of an advertising firm, a sixteen year old schoolboy from Kingston in Surrey, a professional organist, several children, a hat manufacturer, two nuns from a convent, four girl secretaries, the head of a shipping firm, a Q.C., a bank manager, an Australian couple, two Mary Quant assistants, the storeman of an I.C.I. factory, and a member of a pop group. You can understand why the gain is mutual.

Unfortunately an author is not able to live on attention alone. Hence the time we have spent with callers, pleasant and informative as it may have been, has not proved to be a practical way of earning a living. Perhaps we should set up a stall for books, and another stall for Jeannie's paintings and drawings and treat this side of our lives in strict commercial fashion. Such a prospect, however, does not please us. Neither of us enjoys selling our wares. We are poor at doing so. Jeannie, this summer, arranged a number of her paintings in her hut in the wood, but we never succeeded in persuading anyone to look at them. We failed because we adopted the soft sell technique, not the hard sell. We preferred it that way. We therefore hinted that Jeannie had pictures to sell . . . but nobody took the hint; and the only picture she sold was one that I bought myself at the end of the summer. A captivating oil of Lama.

Nor did I do much better. I also hinted. I hinted that I had hard cover copies of my books (not paperbacks) which I would be happy to sign, murmuring that such books would make as good a holiday present as any Midland-made Cornish memento in one of the 'Gifte Shoppes'. Sometimes the information was welcome, at other times there was dead silence. More often I never hinted anything at all. I felt it was out of place to do so. I would instead listen to remarks like: 'It takes so long to get your books from the library,

Mr Tangye . . . I always have to wait *six months* at least.'
Or: 'When I get your books from the library, I spend
hours copying out those passages I like best, before returning
them.' Or: 'When does your new book come out in paperback? I'm *so* looking forward to reading it.' A paperback
earns me 2d a copy. A single hardcover copy in a library
may be read by scores of people, but the author is only paid
the royalty for that one copy.

Yes, despite these financial disadvantages, there are
rewards beyond price. An author who writes about his own
way of life will only have response from those who are on
the same wavelength. It is similar to direct contact with
people. Some you like immediately, some you cannot abide;
some instinctively understand you, some obviously have
nothing in common with you. I cannot abide, for instance,
languid people who are devoid of enthusiasm, people who
avoid facts which interfere with their preconceived opinions,
and people who are ruled by their intellects instead of their
hearts. Nor, for that matter, can I abide professional critics
in any sphere who, like tired roués, no longer find an interest
in anything normal. Such people are unlikely to visit Minack.
Instead, those who have come here have in many instances
kept in touch with us afterwards, and our lives have been
enriched by their friendship.

We were now also in the season of Fêtes, Carnivals, and
Galas; and our special interest, of course, concerned the
festivities of St Buryan and Lamorna. St Buryan has a
splendid village Playing Field, founded and developed by
the local people; and every summer there are two days of
sports and gaieties to celebrate their achievement. Penny
and Fred have a standing invitation to attend, and it is a
pity that they have never done so; but the three-mile road
to the village is narrow and winding, and cars travel fast
along it, and the donkeys, even in our lane, have the habit
of turning broadside on when they see a car approaching.
Thus a journey to St Buryan entailed a risk. There was no
such risk in going to the Gala at Lamorna. We would be able
to reach the field where it was taking place without walking
on a busy road except for a few yards. Or that is what we
thought.

The Gala was in aid of the Lamorna Village Hall Fund; and yellow posters had for some days been displayed in the area, pasted on barn doors, garden walls and the trunks of trees, proclaiming that Jeannie and I were opening the Gala at 2.30 p.m. 'Accompanied by PENNY AND FRED THE DONKEYS.' It sounded easy. All the four of us had to do was to arrive punctually at the appointed place, and the Gala could proceed. All four of us. But supposing two of us chose to be obstinate? Supposing, on the afternoon concerned, two of us wanted to go elsewhere? Or roll in the dust just before we were due to leave? Or supposing, given the good luck of arriving at the Gala, two of us decided to be temperamental? And brayed during the speeches?

Jeannie and I were apprehensive. True the donkeys had always behaved in exemplary fashion at Fred's birthday parties, but these had taken place in the security of Minack, where they were the hosts in a familiar meadow. Even so, such occasions could cause us concern. Anyone, I think, would feel concern if they saw children happily and fearlessly playing around the legs of a donkey. Yet both Penny and Fred accepted such games quite calmly. We were only concerned in case at some stage their patience might be momentarily exhausted. When children were about, therefore, we were always on watch, asking the children to move away whenever necessary. It would be more difficult to watch them at the Gala; and it would be the first time they had ever appeared together in so public a place. The Gala, therefore, would be both an adventure and a test. Their reputations would be at stake.

This also meant that their appearance had to be elegant, and it was fortunate that their coats were now in full summer glory. It is strange how long it takes a donkey to rid itself of a winter coat . . . all through May, June and July, there were woolly patches on both Penny and Fred, giving them both a moth eaten look; and it was to no avail that I combed and groomed them. But the patches had gone now, and the coats were in magnificent condition, Penny a shining black, Fred a glossy chestnut; and all that was now necessary to have them ready for the Gala was a pedicure.

A pedicure suggests a gentle event, and so it should be if the donkeys are in an amiable mood. The hoof of a donkey grows quickly and during the summer a pedicure is necessary every six weeks. A neglected hoof is a sad sight. When Penny first came to Minack, each hoof was elongated and curved upwards at the end, so that she could only walk on her heels. This one-time neglect has made her scared whenever her turn for a pedicure comes round; and although she is normally the most docile of donkeys she will, if in particular nervous mood, behave badly when our black-smith tries to perform his task.

Our blacksmith, Kenny Male from St Buryan, is a patient man, an expert in handling horses and donkeys, and we are lucky to have such a person who is understanding enough to cope with Penny's tantrums. On this occasion Penny was calm as he dealt with each front hoof, cutting and filing them until they both looked trim; but she became highly excited when he tried to catch hold of a back leg. It is not a job I would at any time like to do myself. Penny was wildly lashing out while Geoffrey struggled to hold her by the halter, and while Kenny waited coolly for the moment when he had a chance of seizing a leg. This, in due course, he succeeded in doing. First one leg, then the other, each hoof receiving its trimming; and when at last the task was completed and Penny realised her ordeal was over, she looked as happy as someone who had finished a tough session at the dentist. We rewarded her with a large carrot.

It was at this precise moment while Penny was munching and I was leading Fred by the halter towards Kenny, that a party of teenagers appeared, headed by a schoolteacher. They came from London and were exploring this part of Cornwall; and the timing of their arrival at Minack was heaven-sent. For Fred had been observing the tantrums of his mother; and had no doubt been saying to himself, 'what she can do I can do better.' The sight of the audience, how-ever, quite changed his mind. Fred responds to an audience as a film star responds to a mob of fans; and although, a moment before, he may have been prepared to be mis-chievous, he now saw the opportunity of showing off his sweet nature. This is the role he most enjoys playing. The

137

role which provokes people to murmur: 'Oh, isn't he a dear!' and: 'Such a darling, your Fred,' and: 'He's so handsome!'

Hence Kenny had no trouble at all. The audience gathered along the small fence which separated them from the spot where the pedicure was about to take place, made flattering remarks as Fred quietly advanced, led on the halter by me, and watched admiringly as Fred put on his act. An act which received praise from all of us.

'Do you want my right hoof first, or my left?'

Kenny wanted neither.

'Oh, you're starting with my back left . . . Don't worry . . . I'll keep still.'

The performance was soon over, and Fred accepted the applause. He had been admired once again, and now he shared with his mother the smartest hooves in the district. The donkeys were ready for the Gala.

We had allowed three quarters of an hour to reach the field. It was a hot summer's day, and the lane was dusty, and we would have been wearing casual summer clothes had we been taking the donkeys for a normal walk. The occasion, however, required formality. We had to look as smart as the donkeys for whom we had bought two white halters; and so I was wearing a grey suit and well polished shoes, and Jeannie a pale yellow sleeveless dress with gloves to match. She had, however, taken the precaution of asking Geoffrey to go ahead in the car, taking her pair of Raynes shoes and matching handbag with him; and thus along the lane she wore ordinary shoes which she would change in the car park. A good idea. She would look at herself in the car mirror, and arrive at the Gala cool and collected, having joined me and the donkeys again at the gate.

First, however, we had to reach the car park; and after coming to the end of the dusty lane, we turned right, not on to the main road but on to a narrow lane which led to two farms, a Methodist Chapel, and the Menwinnion Hotel which was once the home of my dear friend Jimmy Williams, the remarkable Elephant Bill. His book about the elephants of the Fourteenth Army in Burma is an immortal one. He and the animals in his life shared an intuition

138

for each other; and he was a man, if you were suffering from animal grief, whom you would dearly love to meet; and I remember that the day after Monty died Jeannie met him in Penzance. She returned calmer to Minack.

The four of us were approaching Menwinnion when Geoffrey appeared in the lane with Philip and Julie his children. They had walked up from the car park to meet us. This was a relief. The donkeys were now in virgin land as far as they were concerned; and they were showing signs of excitement. *What* was the Chapel building? *Who* lived in the two cottages? *Why* can't we go up that turning which is signposted to Tregurno, or that other one to Boleigh? The sight of Geoffrey, therefore, gave us confidence; and the sight of Julie in a pretty pink checked dress with a bow in her hair, and Philip in white shirt and shorts gave us the atmosphere of the Gala to come. We began to rid ourselves of the anxiety which always attacks some of those who feature in such an activity; and, as I walked beside him, I gave Fred a pat. 'You'll enjoy this,' I said.

We passed Menwinnion, where the tarmac lane ended, and then on we went down the south side of Lamorna Valley, down a narrow footpath called Rocky Lane until the car park came into view on our left. 'We've timed it perfectly,' I said to Jeannie, looking at my watch, 'you go ahead and change your shoes. We're due in five minutes. Geoffrey will lead Penny.'

Five minutes later we were in trouble.

I should, of course, have foreseen the situation. I should have made a reconnaisance of the Gala field beforehand, and noted that to reach the field surrounded by Lamorna woods, a wooden ridge had to be crossed. A wooden bridge! As soon as I saw it I knew what would happen . . . the donkeys reached it, looked at it, and came to a full stop.

'Donkeys,' I cried out in anguish, 'please, please don't let us down!'

Nothing I said, nothing we did would make them budge. We cajoled, we tugged, we pushed. The Gala visitors laughed, the organisers looked serious, and Jeannie and I were distraught.

'Donkeys,' I implored them again, 'everyone is waiting

139

for you. For goodness sake MOVE!'

They never did.

We had instead to turn back ignominiously, and make a detour round by the main road, then across two fields, and over a bramble-covered patch of waste land. Jeannie in her smart shoes. The donkeys revelling in such a new and interesting walk.

I began my speech thirty-five minutes late.

FOURTEEN

The behaviour of the donkeys at the Gala was impeccable.
They listened attentively to my speech. They were unperturbed by the noise and the games played around them. They
politely walked round the field time after time, with children
on their backs. They posed for photographs with the
patience of professional models. They were friendly towards a fine horse called Neptune and a little pony called
Tucker who were also helping everyone to enjoy the afternoon. There was no trouble at all at the Gala. Only the
wooden bridge caused trouble. Once again, when we left,
they refused to cross it; and back across the fields to the
main road we had to go.

I was, therefore, relieved when finally we returned to

Minack, so relieved that I rewarded the donkeys by taking a shovel to the kitchen garden and digging half a basket of carrots. This was an excessive amount, enough for a week, but there was sense behind my extravagance. I had reason to believe that they would be restless after such an afternoon of excitement, that they would be expecting us to pay them further attention; and that unless I did something drastic they would hee-haw their way through the evening. Such a prospect I could not bear. I had had enough of donkeys for the day. I wanted peace; and I reckoned that half a basket of carrots would provide it. I was correct.

I do not enjoy making speeches, and I make very few. Some people, however, delight to stand on a platform with upturned faces in front of them. Such an occasion offers a pleasant illusion of power and self-importance, and as the time of the speech draws near they experience excitement instead of dread. Let me not deprive such people, I usually say to myself when I am invited to open this or that, of their pleasure. Let one of them endure that moment after the speech when one yearns to ask: 'Was it all right?' Let one of them suffer lugubrious comment, fortunately not often overheard by the speaker concerned: 'He was not as good as so-and-so last year.' Let one of them open this or that, not me.

Speechmaking, except for the confident, is a painful business; and Jeannie shares my view. One summer she was invited to open a swimming Gala at Mousehole and, like the rest of us, she was kept awake at night worrying over the speech she would make. The morning of the Gala arrived, a hot August morning, and she went down to the rocks for a bathe. Once there she used the sea as an audience and she stood, a slim sylph-like figure, on a boulder close to the waves repeating the speech over and over again until she had learnt it by heart. Unfortunately the speech was never heard by anyone else, and her agony of the past few weeks was wasted. The microphone at the Gala went dead as soon as she began.

As for myself, as for my speech at the Lamorna Gala, I hurried through it oblivious that during the course of it I made a bloomer. I had urged that the Cornish should resist

142

big business interests from across the Tamar, that Lamorna Vally must remain for all time a true example of old Cornwall. Inoffensive rhetoric, I thought, until a kindly resident of the valley approached me after I had finished. 'You have forgotten,' he said with a smile, 'that eighty per cent of us who live in Lamorna are "foreigners".' Yes, I had forgotten. Perhaps the reason is that the 'foreigners' concerned are so pleasant that they appear to belong to the valley.

It is no use believing, however, that life in the country spares you discordancy with others. We have the usual problems of human relationships; and though we may be on happy terms with most, there will always be occasional times when we may have misunderstandings with one person or another. I had, for instance, such a misunderstanding with the elderly gentleman who bought the neighbouring farm, including the cottage where Jane once lived. The gentleman came from the north, and he had a determined manner. The previous owner, a Cornishman, had a herd of Guernseys, and grew potatoes and daffodils; and from him we once rented the two acres of cliff land. The new owner did not follow this pattern of farming. He had a fine herd of beef cattle instead. He also kept the three cottages of Pentewan, empty.

The first misunderstanding I had with him concerned half a ton of Magnificence daffodil bulbs which were still in one of the meadows of my old tenancy of the Pentewan cliff I has foolishly believed that I would be able to dig them in my own good time and transfer them to Minack land. Legally, however, they were no longer mine. My new neighbour had bought them along with the farm. Hence all Jeannie and I could do, daffodil season after daffodil season, was to watch them bust into yellow from our side of the hedge (the blooms were never picked commercially). It was an infuriating experience, and costly too; for they were worth £30 or more a year. But the elderly gentleman has left the area now, and the bulbs are back at Minack.

The second misunderstanding I had with him concerned the coastal footpath. There has always been confusion about the footpath along this part of the coast; and even today there is no official one. True the authorities have drawn up

143

its route and have legal powers to enforce it; but such powers are not easily enforced when a landlord is determined to resist them. This means delay and the coastal path in this area has been delayed for years. Hikers could cross Minack land along a path I had marked, but there was no marked path on my neighbour's land; and hikers there were not welcome.

I had, however, a certain sympathy with his attitude. Hikers once left a gate open, and his herd of beef cattle nearly went over the cliff as a result; and he was also subjected to the tactless manners of footpath propagandists. Footpath propagandists are inclined to behave like little dictators. They sally forth from the towns, armed with maps, aiming to trace long forgotten footpaths. These forgotten footpaths were used in bygone days by a farm-worker, perhaps, walking from his cottage to the farm, or by a family going to church, or by the postman. Such paths have no place in these modern days of hikers. A footpath propagandist, therefore, who bossily tells a farmer that a public footpath of long ago passes through his farm-yard or, across a field which is cropped with broccoli, or where a stone hedge keeps cattle from straying, is certain to be unpopular. Indeed the footpath propagandist is only doing a disservice to his cause. He is encouraging the farmer to be awkward. The farmer, after all, is trying to earn a living on his land. The hiker is only passing by.

The manner of mapping footpaths should be brought up-to-date. Too much goodwill is being lost by this emphasis on old footpaths. Indeed, a farmer or landlord, should be invited when necessary to suggest a path over his land. The planning should be done in a spirit of co-operation. Hikers would then be able to enjoy their walks, footpath propagandists would stop looking for trouble, and farmers would have their privacy.

The coastal path that I have marked over Minack land proves this point. Hikers obediently follow it, do not stray away from it, and are glad that it is there. Not that there are many hikers . . . perhaps ten a week during the summer. But this marked path meant also that I was encouraging the hikers to walk across my neighbour's land; and this, in fact, meant encouragement to trespass. I fear my neighbour did not approve of such behaviour, and so this was the cause of our second misunderstanding. Yet I do not believe that the fault was his. Had he been asked, not ordered, to co-operate with the footpath planners, he would have done so.

There was also the complication of the lighthouse. The lighthouse had been erected on his land soon after the wreck of a Spanish ship, the *Juan Ferrer*, a mile or so up the coast; a five hundred ton vessel on passage from Bordeaux to Cardiff with a mixed cargo of onions, cedar plywood, and thousands of chestnut stakes, which went on the rocks one early foggy morning. Minack was chosen as the head-quarters of the rescue parties, and so we saw at first hand the chaos which ensued. At first there was only the vaguest idea as to where the vessel had run aground, hours indeed went by between the time the faint May Day signal had been picked up, and the time the vessel was finally dis-covered. In the meantime eleven sailors had been drowned.

There was no public enquiry afterwards such as takes place after a train or airliner disaster, as to why matters had gone so awry; but it was decided to declare that the lack of a lighthouse was the cause. It focused public opinion on something tangible. It diverted people from asking questions.

It is called an automatic lighthouse, but it is only auto-matic in the sense that no one is stationed on the premises. The fog signal, for instance, still requires someone to push a button to start it; and this is performed by an officer of Trinity House five miles *down* the coast at Penzance . . . on the advice of a coastguard five miles *up* the coast at Tol Pedn at Gwennap Head. Hence fog at Tol Pedn results in the fog signal sounding, although visibility in the lighthouse area may be so clear that the Lizard is visible. This is irk-some for those of us who have to listen to it ashore. More-over the site of the lighthouse is ill chosen. The site is so far within Mount's Bay that the fog signal is often driven inland instead of out to sea, because foggy weather almost always comes in from the south; and so when a wind is blowing, a sea rushing noisily against a boat, the fog signal isn't heard by a boat a mile or so up the coast. The fog signal, indeed, is an anachronism in this age of electronics; and our particular fog signal exists only as a reminder of eleven Spanish seamen whose lives might have been saved.

Meanwhile the lighthouse has provided an indirect obstacle to the coastal path. Trinity House put up a noticeboard on my neighbour's land close to our boundary, at the spot where the coastal path would normally run; and the notice on the board was deceptive. It read: THE PUBLIC IS PROHIBITED FROM ENTERING THE LIGHTHOUSE OR ANY PART OF THE LAND ADJOINING THE LIGHTHOUSE. BY ORDER OF THE CORPORATION OF TRINITY HOUSE.

This suggested that Trinity House had some control of the land when, in fact, it only owns a strip of land on either side of the lighthouse which is some distance from the notice-board. Confusion, as a result, among coastal path hikers who often came to me to complain; and complain too about the strands of barbed wire that run along the boundary, and which my neighbour had fixed as a protection against straying cattle. Or straying donkeys for that matter. Penny and Fred often grazed in the adjoining meadow and once, after a footpath propagandist had cut the wire, they ended up by the gate at Pentewan cottages.

Occasionally the complaints were made aggressively. One day two men and a woman arrived at the door of the cottage saying they had torn their pants on the barbed wire, that this must be my fault, that I was one of those who tried to stop the enjoyment of the public, and that when they returned home after their holiday they would lodge a complaint with the hiker association to which they belonged. All this without asking me what the true situation might be. I would have been happy to explain the reason for the barbed wire, the Trinity House notice and so on; but they were determined to vent their feelings on someone, and so they chose me. I knew, however, their type, and so I didn't argue. They belonged to that intellectual race who are so burdened with the knowledge of other people's rights, so supposedly liberal in their thinking, that they have no room in their minds for truth.

The same evening I was on the bridge and saw Daisy for

146

the first time for some weeks. She was in the stable meadow near to the hedge bordering the lane, a small grey figure intent on some activity in the couch grass; and when her interest waned she looked up at me, too far away for me to see her eyes, just her head facing towards me; and then she began to walk across the meadow, a slow walk towards the cemetery field. And then I forgot about her because Jeannie came to me and said that Boris was squatting on the grass by his pond, and he didn't appear to want to move; and she was frightened that something was wrong.

He had been outside the cottage door for most of the day. Normally he would only come up to the door to receive some special delight from Jeannie or me, stay ten minutes or so, then plod away down the path of grey chippings; and during his brief stay we would make our customary remarks to him.

'Boris, old boy, what are you up to?'

'Now, Boris dear, you've had *plenty*.'

'Dear Boris I'll walk back with you . . .'

But for the past few days he had been staying close to the door as if he had special reasons to want our company; and he annoyed Lama by doing so. Lama was always on guard in case, as she passed him, he had a nip at her tail; and she would eye him warily as she approached the door, then rush past him at speed. It was imagination on her part, of course, that he would harm her; or perhaps it was only a game that she was playing, a ruse to enliven for a minute or so old Boris's day. There they were, the two strays who had come into our lives; the one who had been scheduled to provide a dinner, the other who might have been wild for ever. Both had had a decisive effect on our future. And I wanted neither when first they arrived on the scene.

I went down to the pond with Jeannie, but Boris was no longer squatting there. He was on his way to his house, and there seemed to be nothing wrong with him because he was pausing occasionally and pushing his beak into the new mown grass. We waited until he reached the door, then we bade him good night and shut it.

Back in the cottage Jeannie went to turn the bath on and

147

I heard her call out that there wasn't any water. This was a routine happening now that summer was ending, the springs low. A. P. Herbert was staying with us once at this time of the year, and I remember an occasion when he advanced towards me, pretending to be a sailor marching across the quarter deck.

'I have to report, sir,' he said, saluting, 'that the pumps are sucking.'

Usually the electric pump turns on automatically when the water has reached a certain low in the tank, a hundred-gallon tank which stands beside the well and the pump; and up comes the water from thirty feet down. When the springs are low, however, the bottom of the well only holds forty gallons, and even this small amount takes five hours to gather. Hence I have to switch on the pump manually, and wait four minutes or so beside the tank until the water starts to splutter out of the pipe, and I know the well is empty. Sometimes I walk away after I have started the pump, day-dreaming about some matter; and I proceed to forget all about it until ten, twenty, thirty minutes later I suddenly shout: 'The pump!' . . . and I race away to switch it off. By then it is pumping air, and so a tedious task is the penalty of my forgetfulness. I have to prime the pump when I next use it; and this means using a watering can and labouriously pouring the water down the pipe until its level also fills the pump, and the air is driven out, and the pump can operate again.

That summer evening I had no need to prime it. I switched on, and stood there waiting until the water splashed into the tank. It was dark now, and the stars had come into their own, and I saw above me the bunched cluster of the Pleiades. I first consciously observed them when I lived on my South Sea island of Toopua; and they were directly above me then, as they were now at Minack. I hadn't changed much, I found myself thinking. I did not feel any older, any wiser. I still had self-doubt which would lead me into making a move which was against my interest. I still believed you were a lucky person if you could be happy on your own; and that such people were able to hear the whispers as well as the shouts. I still believed, therefore, that peace of mind

148

could only come from within yourself; and that no outside agency would ever be able to provide it for you.

Nor did my views on people differ much. The sophisticated in London still lived lives of perpetual unfulfilment. I was still surprised by the ease with which people made promises without any intention of carrying them out. I still marvelled at the conceit of those who seemed always certain their opinions were correct. My instinct was still to like everyone at the first meeting. I still believed that courage and kindness lay beneath the surface of the majority. I still admired those with good manners. I was still saddened at the way people were forced to sacrifice their integrity in the cause of self-preservation.

But there were new factors in my life since those days in Toopua, and obviously they must have affected me in other ways. A war had come and gone, and I had survived, and every day of my life I was grateful. Awareness of the luck of it came to me in sudden moments, reminding me that I was one of those who lived on borrowed time. Such moments offered other thoughts as well. I remember a pretty secretary in my office who fell in love with a Dane serving in the R.A.F.; and within a month of their being married he was killed. Of course such an incident was repeated a thousand, thousand times during the war so that it became a normality. Yet there are moments, and this was one of them as I stood there up by the well, that I reflected about that girl, and those who suffered like her, wondering whether the intensity of her love all those years ago has ever been quelled. So I was grateful too for this . . . for the fact that I hadn't carried that kind of desolate memory through my life.

And since that night I first became aware of the Pleiades, Jeannie had come into my life; and I had learnt there were no rules to follow in a happy marriage. Only that both of you must feel that you have freedom and that you are not chained to a conventional routine. Habit is what must be avoided. Every day must bring the unexpected so that, in a way, you remain strangers anxious to discover each other. All my years with Jeannie have been an adventure; the frivolous, glamorous times of London . . . or the first night at Minack when we slept on a mattress on the floor while

149

the rain dripped through a hole in the roof. The companion-
ship I have had with her has had its warmth through the
unexpected. I am unable to take her for granted. She is
elusive, provocative, feminine, always ready to make a sacrifice, showing faith in reality by not running away from it,
yet always on the verge of chasing wild, imaginative Celtic
dreams. No dullness with Jeannie.

The water in the pipe began to splutter, and I switched
off the pump; and as I did so a flight of curlews flew over
the wood uttering their sad, romantic cries. An owl
answered from somewhere near Boris's house; and from
across the valley I heard a fox barking. Lights of houses
speckled at intervals along the coastline of the Lizard, and
close to those of Porthleven, I could see the red lights of
helicopters hovering like fireflies above the naval air station
of Culdrose. It was warm, and the night air was fragrant
with the night-scented stock and the tobacco plants. I could
hear the hum of a trawler, and then I saw her starboard light
rounding Carn Barges; and far out on the horizon there
was a tiny smudge of light, a liner no doubt though there
was no telling which way she was sailing. I went back to the
cottage and saw the shadow of Lama waiting for me at the
corner by the water butt. I bent down to stroke her but before
I was able to touch her she dashed away towards the porch.
Bedtime, she had decided.

Next morning I went in my usual casual way to open the
door of Boris's house; and I gave him my customary greeting: 'Good morning, old boy. Have you had a good night?'
I noted him in the corner, and took no more notice because
in recent weeks he had been slow to move out. Not like the
old days when he behaved like a greyhound waiting to be
released from a race trap . . . then he would bounce out of
his house in a flurry of wagging tail feathers, accompanied
by a cacophony of hisses. He was eager to take part in the
day.

Breakfast was to be on the bridge, and I went up there
and waited for Jeannie to bring me two boiled eggs and
coffee; and she brought them on a tray with a saucer of
milk for Lama who was sitting close to my feet, gently purring. Two of the gulls were on the roof, and when they saw

Jeannie with the tray they began to squawk for their breakfast; and so she had to go back and cut them some bread. I
thought it was going to be an ordinary day, and I revelled
in the prospect of it. The tomatoes were virtually finished;
and so there was no work for me to do in that direction.
Perhaps, I said to Jeannie, we might take the donkeys for a
walk along the cliff towards Lamorna; and she thought this
a good idea because there would be blackberries to pick,
and she would be able to make her first jar or two of jam.

I finished my breakfast and went over to talk to the
donkeys who were quietly grazing in the big field above
the cottage; and as I reached them Fred thought I had come
for a game, and suddenly sprinted away. I was about to
chase him when I heard Jeannie shouting, and her voice was
so urgent that I started to run back across the field; and this,
Fred thought, was also part of the game, and as I ran, he
was close behind me.

I found Jeannie in front of the cottage by the rose garden
with Boris beside her swaying, as if he were unable to keep
his balance. As I reached them, Boris stumbled away towards his pond, plunged into it, and began beating his wings
on the water. After a minute he flapped his way out, and
collapsed on the grass. I thought as I watched him, that I
was watching him die. Then he got to his feet again and
before we had time to stop him, he half flew across the grey
chippings towards the corner of the cottage, then up the
short steep path to the water butt, and right to the door.
The route he had taken every day of his life with us at
Minack. There he was in his favourite place, waiting for
something that only instinct made him expect.

We carried him to the small greenhouse, and made a nest
for him in a bundle of hay; and we had a vet out to see
him; and we watched over him and cared for him during
the following two nights and days.

Then quietly at midday on a Tuesday, he died.

151

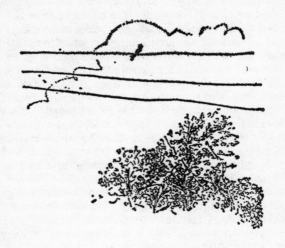

FIFTEEN

The swallows were leaving. The electricity cable which ran
from pole to pole through a gap in the wood, up the valley
to the farms at the top, provided the resting place of the
travellers from up country. Long lines of swallows would
settle for a while, cleaning themselves, twittering, dashing
away to skim the fields and moorland, then back again.
They would stay for a few hours or so, longer sometimes,
and then off towards Lands End and, if the wind was fair,
straight on across the sea to France or the Basque country,
even a long flight to Portugal. What parts of this country had
they come from, what old houses of England had been their
homes during the summer? I was saddened by the gay manner with which they were leaving. No British winter for us.

We want the sun of South Africa. Let's fly away as soon as possible.

Our second brood, however, were still in the barn; and I had observed that, as always, there was one more advanced than the others, a bossy young swallow with white shirt front rimming the nest, seizing the best flies brought by his parents. We called him Pip, and the other two shy ones, Squeak and Wilfred. Any day now they would be learning to fly, and they had not much time to spare if they were to be strong enough to start on their journeys before the autumn gales began.

From the bridge we watched other travellers, the spotted flycatchers and the warblers, training our field-glasses upon them so that their bright eyes were so close that it seemed we were watching their minds at work. The spotted fly-catchers were easy to recognise. They would choose a branch of a tree, perch there quite still, a perky little bird with the shape of a robin, then suddenly dart at a passing fly twisting and turning to catch it, and then back to his perch. to await another. Sometimes we had a dozen or more around Minack, waiting for a wind to help them on their way to Africa.

I am at a loss, however, when trying to identify the warblers. I have various bird books, and I scan them closely, and notice how confidently the writers discriminate between a Garden Warbler, a Chiff Chaff, a Wood Warbler, a Willow Warbler, and other kinds of warblers . . . but they all look the same to me. I can recognise a Chiff Chaff, that's easy. I just listen to his chiff chaff call, then observe the busy hopping of the bird from branch to branch of a tree. Others of the warbler family, however, just baffle me. I have observed them from the bridge darting among the leaves of the apple tree which I planted years ago in the grass in front of the bridge; and among the leaves of the blackthorn in the three-cornered meadow to the right of the bridge. Secretive birds, always on the move, and I have to be smart to keep them in view as they skip around picking up grubs from the leaves; and then after a week or two they are gone again, setting course for the savanna country around the Congo forests three thousand miles away. But to

153

what branches of the warbler family did they belong? Alas, Jeannie and I gave up trying to find out. We just watched them and marvelled, and in so doing I remembered my father's advice.

My father, when I was a child, warned me never to ask questions about sights that were naturally beautiful. Accept them, he used to say, as a means of exciting your emotions but do not try to analyse why. I do not suppose he expected me to take this advice too literally, but I have learnt to understand what he was trying to tell me. Those who were guided by the heart, he used to argue, were closer to the truth than sceptics who were always trying to satisfy their intellects. Pleasure, in fact, should be for enjoyment and not for critical investigation. An out of date view, of course, in this technological age. Yet it is a view that still has substance for some of us.

I was aware, on the other hand, that an idle time of staring and contemplation and living in the present, could only be justified if you had earned it. I knew, for instance, that our own pleasure this summer had been derived from experiences of things past, by efforts laboriously made, by all the failures, by successes which had suddenly pushed us forward without pushing us too far. Thus we had been able to pause, and live a dream without being so far from reality to deceive ourselves that it could last forever.

We still had to earn a living in professions, for instance, which had no means of countering rising costs by obtaining rising returns. Booksellers were closing down in many parts of the country. As flower growers and tomato growers we could not agitate like farmers for increased controlled prices in the annual government price review. The prices we received were half what they were ten years ago, and yet we were enforced by law to pay the rising costs imposed upon us. No wonder there is a drift of labour from the land. There isn't the money available to pay the wages.

Thus the summer had nearly ended, and our basic problems remained as real as ever though I did not allow myself to be concerned by them. There were the September pleasures still to enjoy, and I sat on the bridge indulging in such minor delights as the aroma of blackberries stewing. Most

154

days we went blackberrying accompanied by the donkeys; and sometimes there was rivalry when one of them tried to reach a juicy clump before we had noticed it ourselves. Jam was the main object of our blackberrying. Jeannie aimed to make twenty pounds.

There were, too, such minor delights as watching the young green woodpecker devouring the ants that crawled by the wall where we fed the donkeys in the field above the cottage. Or listening to the hum of the bees among the brilliant red flowers of the fuchsia and among the honeysuckle opposite the cottage door. Or watching Daisy pass across the stable meadow. Or seeing the swallows still tirelessly diving in and out of the barn door. Or being deceived by a patch of red brown bracken into thinking it was a fox sunning itself. Or seeing an oil rig being towed across the horizon towards the Lizard, the size of a vast city office block, scaringly incongruous in a shipping lane. I shouted to Geoffrey when I saw it, and after looking through his field-glasses, he said with a Cornish-man's native sense: '*That* would make a good wreck.'

We continued to have visitors, all kinds of visitors. A young man arrived who was a male nurse in a London hospital, and he enthused us with the account of his dedication. Another was a young musician from Chester who had come to see us in other summers. Then there was an Australian who called, bringing with her messages from her neighbours in Melbourne. A Canadian family on a world tour arrived in a Daimler, and when I first saw it coming down the lane I thought to myself that it was too wide to get over Monty's Leap. It survived . . . but an American couple in a Rolls-Royce a couple of days later became stuck. The sharp dip into the water bed of the Leap was too much for the exhaust pipe. It became wedged against the lane surface, and it required cunning work on Geoffrey's part to free it.

People came and asked for Boris, and when we told them what had happened, there was a silence, and a child who had come with her parents inquired: 'Did he just fly far away?' We could not bear to see his empty pond after he had died, so we emptied it and broke up the cement of the basin, and buried him there; and we planted the London

Pride on the surface, the same London Pride which edged the rose garden and upon which he liked to doze. And there were two girls who came, and they were so concerned that they went away, unknown to us, to search the area for another muscovy drake to take his place. They returned in due course with a baby drake in a box; and we had to explain to them that their kindly thought was misplaced. We did not want a substitute for Boris.

Lama had special visitors of her own. She has, in the past, even had cats brought along by holidaymakers to visit her. I admire the nerve of such people who take their cats on holiday. I have a recurring nightmare of taking Lama to London by car, and the height of the nightmare is when I am in a traffic jam in Shaftesbury Avenue, and Lama manages to escape from the car and then disappears into the side streets of Soho. I wake up moaning. This September a fine tabby called Sammy came to Minack with his owner who was a district nurse in Croydon. She and her husband were holidaymaking in a tent near Lands End, and Sammy took his unnatural surroundings quite for granted. Sammy was an experienced traveller. He daily accompanied the district nurse on her busy rounds back home.

Then there was a charming elderly French lady called Madame Madeleine Boniface who came specially on a two-day visit to Penzance from Paris in order to meet Lama. A great admirer of Colette she considered that both Monty and Lama were in the tradition of the cats of Colette; and so she felt impelled to make Lama's acquaintance.

On the morning she called I had looked through the window of the lane side of the barn and I had seen that Pip for the first time had left the nest, and was perched on an old windbreak which was leaning against the inside barn wall. This indeed was a sign of summer's end. Squeak and Wilfred would soon follow, and after fluttering around in the nursery for a day or two, they would be flying outside, and soon after, they would be joining the great concourse on the way to the south. All these months of watching the swallows behaving as if they owned Minack; and now the sky around the barn would be empty. At least the donkeys would have the place for themselves again.

It is not easy, from the bridge, to see a figure in the lane near Monty's Leap for it is hidden by the low leafy branches of the elms bordering the lane, and this means it is also in the shadow. If, therefore, someone is standing there hesitantly, my attention to the presence is first drawn by the movement of feet. Madame Boniface, in this case, had come by bus from Penzance to the end of the lane, walked the mile distance to the Leap; and then had lost her nerve. She was about to return when I observed her shuffling feet, and went down from the bridge to ask her whether I could be of any help. She thereupon confessed her mission.

Unfortunately Lama, as the summer months passed by, had become increasingly indifferent to adulation. At first, in the spring there was a freshness in being told how beautiful she looked. The flattery was stimulating, enhanced the pleasure of her days, and indeed there was excitement as to who might be arriving next to pay the praise which was her due. Of course she had her disappointments, occasions when she sauntered nonchalantly towards a visitor who, unknown to her, disliked cats; and who had come to see the donkeys, even ourselves, instead. Such moments of embarrassment, however, were quickly covered up by swift action on the part of Jeannie or myself. Acutely sensing the atmosphere, we would gather up Lama in our arms and hurry her indoors.

These occasions, nonetheless, were rare. She was, in fact, so much in demand, so repeatedly photographed, picked up, hugged, stroked, played with, innocently teased by children, and generally made a fuss of, that by August a blasé mood could be noted in her behaviour. By September this mood had become glaringly apparent. Some admirer would approach her with suitable friendly noises and she would forthwith turn her black silky posterior towards the admirer and march away, leaving us to make the excuses. Sometimes, however, I felt she had good reasons for such rudeness. There was an inclination on the part of many of her admirers to inquire her age. There she would be in the most obliging fashion coping with the hugging, the clicking cameras, and the contrived games when suddenly the remark

157

would be made: 'She must be getting on . . . how old is she now?' Our own tart reply was to say that it was not good manners to ask a lady her age. But this Lama did not think was good enough. Indeed I believe that the frequency of this question throughout the summer was one of the chief causes of her September impatience. What did age matter? Why was everyone so self-conscious about age?

In September she became increasingly inclined to hide. She had nests in various spots around Minack, each of them securing her favour for a while; and although we believed we had mapped them all she was always able to fool us. There was a nest on the wall close to the bridge, a curved cavity of pressed dry grass, a most favourite spot from which, as we sat letting the time go by, we would hear a quiet heave-ho of gentle snores. There was another up by the well, and another by the stream at the bottom of our small orchard, and another high up on the wall which framed our old wooden potato house. This nest was within the territory of the stable meadow which the donkeys used; and Fred knew about it though he was aggravated by the fact it was just out of reach of his enquiring nose.

But it was remarkable how often she was in none of these nests we knew; and we would vainly call her and rush from nest to nest, becoming increasingly irritated, our calls even louder, until at last in our exhaustion we would have to admit to the admirer who had come to see her that she was unavailable. And this is what happened when Madame Boniface called. There was not a sign of her. We spent an hour and a half charging round Minack and there wasn't a miaow in response. Every foot of land we examined. Every section echoed with our calls. She was no longer my favourite cat. I became angry. For after all how often does a one-time wild cat receive a visitor from Paris?

Half an hour after Madame Boniface's departure, Lama appeared. All purrs. So there was only one thing I could do. We shut her in the bedroom. Then I drove to Penzance, found the hotel where Madame Boniface was staying, and brought her back. No trouble this time. Lama was charming.

Three days later I saw Squeak and Wilfred caught in the cobwebs of the alcove by the barn window. Pip was already flying on his own outside, then returning to the barn; but Squeak and Wilfred were just out of the nest. I picked each up in my hand, removed the cobwebs clinging to their wings, then took them to the barn door and let them free. It was the first time they had seen the space of the world, and they left my hand unafraid, and soared into the sky and, though watching them for some clumsy aerobatics, I saw them flying around the stable meadow with the ease of veterans. Two more swallows ready for South Africa.

The sun was still warm, and the school holidays were over, and two days would go by without anyone calling; and Jeannie and I found our minds were at ease, so that, as in the spring, we felt able to picnic on the rocks with a bottle of wine and sandwiches of home-made bread; and feel free of anyone wanting us. The gulls, of course, were still annoyed when they saw us appear. They rose from the rocks, uttering raucous epithets, and we were sorry that we were disturbing them; but the sea and the sky were their kingdom, time too, and there was no reason to feel guilty as they drifted away from Minack rocks.

At night I took a torch to the barn to check the swallows which were roosting there. The parents were the first to go. Pip went next, five days later. Then Squeak four days after him.

I was never happy as to what happened to Wilfred. He was always the weakest. He still came back to the nest a week after Squeak had gone.

Then he too disappeared; and the summer was ended.

END

A selection of bestsellers from Sphere:

FICTION

THE SEVENTH SECRET	Irving Wallace	£2.95 □
CARIBBEE	Thomas Hoover	£3.50 □
THE GLORY GAME	Janet Dailey	£3.50 □
NIGHT WARRIORS	Graham Masterton	£2.95 □
THE DAMNATION GAME	Clive Barker	£3.50 □

FILM & TV TIE-IN

INTIMATE CONTACT	Jacqueline Osborne	£2.50 □
BEST OF BRITISH	Maurice Sellar	£8.95 □
SEX WITH PAULA YATES	Paula Yates	£2.95 □
RAW DEAL	Walter Wager	£2.50 □
INSIDE STORY	Jack Ramsay	£2.50 □

NON-FICTION

HOLLYWOOD A' GO-GO	Andrew Yule	£3.50 □
THE OXFORD CHILDREN'S THESAURUS		£3.95 □
THE MAUL AND THE PEAR TREE	T.A. Critchley & P.D. James	£3.50 □
DUKE: THE LIFE AND TIMES OF JOHN WAYNE	Donald Shepherd & Robert Slatzer	£3.95 □
WHITEHALL: TRAGEDY & FARCE	Clive Ponting	£4.95 □

All Sphere books are available at your local bookshop or newsagent, or can be ordered direct from the publisher. Just tick the titles you want and fill in the form below.

Name _____

Address _____

_____

Write to Sphere Books, Cash Sales Department, P.O. Box 11, Falmouth, Cornwall TR10 9EN

Please enclose a cheque or postal order to the value of the cover price plus:

UK: 60p for the first book, 25p for the second book and 15p for each additional book ordered to a maximum charge of £1.90.

OVERSEAS & EIRE: £1.25 for the first book, 75p for the second book and 28p for each subsequent title ordered.

BFPO: 60p for the first book, 25p for the second book plus 15p per copy for the next 7 books, thereafter 9p per book.

Sphere Books reserve the right to show new retail prices on covers which may differ from those previously advertised in the text elsewhere, and to increase postal rates in accordance with the P.O.